COTTAGE *Style*

Ideas & Projects
for Your World

JERRI FARRIS AND TIM HIMSEL

CREATIVE
PUBLISHING
international

CHANHASSEN, MINNESOTA

www.creativepub.com

CONTENTS

Preface
page 5

Introduction
page 7

Furnishings
page 21

Pillows & Linens
page 49

Mirrors & Frames
page 71

Accents
page 85

Lighting
page 105

Techniques
page 123

Patterns
page 130

Afterword
page 136

Index
page 137

Resources
page 140

PROJECTS

Glass-top Table. 27

Decoupage Tabletop 29

Mirrored Tray Table 33

Drop Leaf Table 35

Five-board Bench 39

Embellished Bookcase 43

Simple Headboard 45

Envelope Pillow 55

Silk Flower Bouquet Pillow. . . . 57

Basket Liner Pillow. 58

Script Pillow. 59

Pieced Pillow 60

Fleece Blanket 63

Embellished Linens 65

Mosaic Mirror 77

Fabric-covered Mirror. 78

Textured Mirror 79

Beadboard Frame 81

Molding-compound Frame 82

Embellished Frame. 83

Spindle Clocks 91

Mantle Clock 92

Half Moon Mantle Clock 95

Floor Cloth. 97

Miniature Wire Table & Chair . 99

Display Shelf 103

Teapot Lamp 111

Teacup Candle 113

Refurbished Chandelier 115

Gilded Candlesticks 119

Baluster Floor Lamp 121

Tim Himsel and Jerri Farris

$\mathcal{P}$REFACE

Cottage Style is a natural addition to the series Tim Himsel and I have spent the last several years developing. The cottage look is wildly popular and absolutely suited to the sort of projects we love to design and build. Even so, I had no idea how much fun this would be, nor how much we would come to love the book and its projects. I also had no idea that developing it would teach me as much about life as it did about decorating.

Once again, I find myself in awe of my friend and creative partner, Tim Himsel. Tim sees remarkable possibilities within the most ordinary of materials and can figure out how to translate those possibilities into realities. He created the graphic design of the book, designed many of the projects, and helped me refine construction details for many of my designs. But even beyond his many talents, I admire the even-tempered way Tim handles the pressures of workloads and deadlines and an occasionally hyper creative partner. Working with him continues to be one of the great blessings of my life.

A group of incredible people helped us put this book together, and we appreciate all their efforts. We'd especially like to mention Sheila Duffy, who made many of the projects, Teresa Henn, who built projects and modeled for the photography, and Randy Austin who built the sets and helped with the projects. Sheila, Teresa, and Randy improved every project they touched and generously shared their time, talents, and ideas. Andrea Rugg and Tate Carlson did an outstanding job with the photography, and John Rajtar presented our work in the best possible light with his superb propping and styling. And this time, it took the combined efforts of Tracy Stanley, Julie Caruso, and Jon Simpson to keep us in line. Thank you, one and all.

Last, but by no means least, Tim and I would like to thank Dorothy Halla-Poe of the Land of Oz Bed and Breakfast, whose home is pictured in several places throughout the book. Dorothy opened not only her home but her heart to us, and we are profoundly grateful on both counts.

Jerri Farris

$\mathscr{I}$NTRODUCTION

To understand cottage style, you first must understand cottages: small, simple houses filled with light, color, and the romantic aura of gracious living. The rooms are intimate and cozy, with the kind of softness that invites the occupants to relax and enjoy themselves. A cottage is emotionally and visually connected to nature, especially the surrounding landscape, which typically includes bountiful gardens.

Close your eyes and imagine a cottage. What do you see?

If you're like most people, the images include the vine-covered cottage from a dozen clichés; maybe the candy-laden trim of a gingerbread house or the thatched roof of the woodcutter's home in a favorite fairy tale. Or perhaps a seaside hideaway. They almost certainly include garden beds and borders, maybe a climbing rose or two. Whatever the specifics of the image may be, it's likely to be highly idealized, a picture of life as we wish it could be. A place where life is practically perfect, where you can count on wicked witches getting their comeuppance, where there's always time to putter in the garden or meander along the beach.

Very few of us live the sort of fairy tale lives conjured up by these images, but still we're attracted to the idea and style of cottages, to their comfort and their romance. What creates that timeless appeal? Why are we still building and decorating cottages and cottage-style homes hundreds of years after their style was first adopted by European nobility trying to imitate the supposedly simpler lives of peasants?

The answer lies in our nature as human beings. You see, our homes describe us. We fill them with our values and personalities, our histories, our hopes, and our dreams. Many of us long for the type of lives promised by cottages. We want to be surrounded by the beauty and ease, the sentiment and connectedness that we associate with them.

Marie Antoinette certainly wasn't a milkmaid and probably could barely imagine the realities of that life, yet at the end of the 18th century she escaped the demands of her royal life by spending time in a specially constructed cottage. Actually, she

had not just a cottage but an entire hamlet built on the grounds of the Palace of Versailles—a place where she could live freely and happily, surrounded by simplicity and the bounty of nature.

Even without Marie Antoinette's resources, even if we don't own a cottage and never will, we can create a cottage atmosphere and enjoy its ambience. No matter where we live, we can bring cottage style into our homes and into our lives if we understand its nature.

Cottage style is graciousness come to life, built on attention to detail and an appreciation of the art of making a house into a home. It creates a connection between outdoors and in, celebrating all of nature, especially gardens and flowers. It is the decorating equivalent of my mother's lifelong insistence that pretty food tastes better.

The interior of a cottage often is composed of layers of possessions and the collected memories of the generations who have lived and loved in it. In that same way, a cottage-style home should showcase the best of a family's history and its heritage. I say "the best," because one of the main features of a cottage is that it's small, and space has to be used effectively. That means weeding out, editing, and recycling from time to time.

The cottage shown on page 6 is the home of Dorothy Halla-Poe, proprietor of the Land of Oz Bed and Breakfast in Bay City, Wisconsin. Dorothy graciously allowed us to photograph some of our projects at her home and in her gardens. She says that with the name Dorothy and a dog named Toto, the theme for her B&B was pretty much a given, but she also says that's not the whole story. "The lesson of the Wizard of Oz is that there's no place like home, and I have always known that.

"There truly is no other place on earth like my home. I love my gardens and my house and my cottage. I love just being here, watching the seasons come and go."

There is no other pace on earth quite like your home, either. Our goal for *Cottage Style* is to help you make your home—wherever and whatever it may be—look and feel like your image of a cottage. So click your heels together three times and let's get started.

COTTAGE RULES:

• **Never buy anything that matches.** This is one of our most important suggestions. The casual, eclectic, *collected* look of a cottage *cannot* evolve from matched sets of furniture or accessories. If you have matching pieces that simply must stay, add slipcovers or paint or additional trim of some sort to differentiate them.

• **Think in layers.** Imagine that your home has been passed down through several generations, each of which has left a layer of furnishings, accessories, and memories.

• **Connect the layers with color.** Choose a color palette (see page 14) and weave it through your rooms.

Medium tones of colors found in gardens often are the most successful.

• **Soften the rooms with fabric.** Find imaginative ways to incorporate fabric, ribbons, lace, and trim in upholstered furniture, pillows, window treatments, skirted tables and so forth.

• **Create a mood with lighting.** Cast a rosy glow with pink lightbulbs or choose lampshades in warm colors; incorporate lots of candles.

• **Bring your imagination out to play.** Romance, whimsy, and humor are the foundation of cottage-style decorating.

Research

It might surprise you, but the first stop I'm going to suggest as you adopt cottage style isn't a fabric store, furniture store, or even the paint department of your local home center. No, the first stop is an office or art supply store to buy a spiral-bound sketch book, 11 × 14" or so, some small scissors, and rubber cement.

The next stop should be a comfortable chair in your own home. Pick a time when you can work uninterrupted for a while. Turn off the phone and the television, curl up comfortably and daydream. Really let your imagination wander. Get out your sketchbook. If you have memories of special cottages, spend some time recalling the things you liked about them. Make notes. Jot down descriptive words. Sketch your memories.

Next, gather magazines of all sorts and cut out pictures that appeal to you. Include images of gardens and natural landscapes as well as room settings and house exteriors. Don't try to make the photos match or go together or follow a plan—just gather images that speak to your spirit and glue them into random collages. This project will take several sessions, but it will be fun—a little bit like paper dolls for grown-ups.

Eventually, patterns will take shape and you'll recognize that materials and colors are repeated throughout your collages. You'll probably find textures, shapes, and themes being repeated, too, but for the first step all you need is a sense of the colors and materials that represent cottages to you.

Planning

Working on one area at a time is much less frustrating and messy and produces more impact than a scattered approach. So, pick a room and spend some time there. Think about how you use the room and whether simple changes or additions could make it more functional or appealing. Consider the furnishings and accessories. Remember that true cottages represent years and years—generations even—of family heritage. They're loved for their character, including their imperfections and idiosyncrasies. It's fine to make changes and improvements, but keep the things you absolutely love, no matter what. Adopting cottage style is not about throwing everything out and starting over from scratch, it's about taking what you have and making it better. You're not building a stage set, you're creating a comfortable home for yourself and your family.

Measure the room carefully, and draw it in your sketchbook. Note the room's dimensions and the size and placement of the doors and windows. As you make decisions, add samples or photographs of the wallpaper, paint, flooring, furnishings, and fabrics that will remain in the room.

Study the wall and ceiling surfaces in your collages and then the ones in your room. Do your walls and ceilings have the character of the images in your collages? Do they showcase

your favorite furnishings and possessions? If so, you're ready to move on. If not, perhaps the walls need shape or texture. What about adding architectural moldings? Don't underestimate the potential impact of crown molding, picture or chair rail moldings, and wide baseboards. Home centers offer a wide range of reasonably priced trim, and it's often one of the best investments you can make in a room. If the walls need more texture, think about adding wainscoting or stucco paint; consider beadboard, car siding, and exposed studs for walls or ceilings. Any of these projects is within the capabilities of most homeowners, and home centers are full of products designed specifically for do-it-yourselfers.

When you're satisfied with your decisions on the walls and ceiling, move to flooring. Think about what you learned from your collages and look at the current flooring. Does it complement the room you're creating? If not, are major changes necessary or can you work with it somehow? Remember that, like the rest of a cottage-style home, the floors don't need to be perfect. Cottages are supposed to have a slightly worn, lived-in look. Painted designs or stencils can revive tired hardwood, and area rugs can cover a multitude of sins on any flooring. If major changes are necessary, consult a contractor or one of the many home improvements guides available at bookstores and libraries everywhere.

Add samples to your sketchbook of any new surfaces, trim, or flooring you've selected.

Color

With the shapes and surfaces selected, it's time to think about color. First, head to your favorite paint retailer and purchase a fan deck of paint samples, usually available for $15 to $20. This may seem like an extravagance, but a fan deck is an investment that will pay for itself over and over.

Back in the room, settle in with your sketchbook and fan deck. The goal here is to choose a color palette—two or three basic colors. Start by studying your collages. Which colors show up repeatedly? Are certain combinations repeated? Which ones make you smile?

Now evaluate the room and the pieces that are staying. What colors do they suggest?

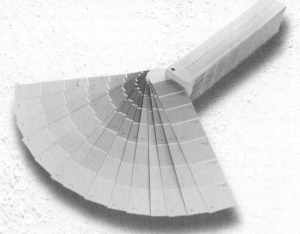

Pull out the fan deck and play with colors until you find a combination that feels right. Lay out the samples in plain sight and live with them for a few days. Put together several groupings of related shades of the basic colors. Look at them at different times of day under a variety of light sources.

When you've decided on your color palette, add samples to your sketchbook. Now take a long look at the room. Do its current colors work with your palette? What others would complement the room's features? Review the samples of any new trim, surfaces, or flooring you've selected. Do they suggest any particular shades? Use your fan deck to select paint for the walls, trim, and even ceilings.

A word of advice before we move on: Don't let yourself get boxed into a corner by trendy colors. Some people decorate by selecting a set of colors and making sure everything in a room is one of those colors. It doesn't take long for everyone to be very tired of those two or three colors, so trends change often and home owners scramble to keep up. That approach is needlessly expensive and time-consuming. It also dates a room almost immediately. For example, endless combinations

of teal, burgundy, and rose peg a room to the mid-1980's just as surely as huge shoulder pads on a silk dress.

Every color includes an almost infinite variety of shades. Use them. Pick a basic color palette and let subtle shading provide variety, interest and character. If evergreen is included in your color palette (as it well might be, given the connections between nature and cottage style), use it plus a variety of the hundreds of shades of green found in nature.

With your palette selected, you're ready for action. If you decided to add or replace wall or ceiling surfaces, trim, or flooring, pull out your tools or call a contractor and get to work. Again, I suggest you consult a home improvement book regarding specific projects and work sequences. If all you need to do is paint, get that done before you start buying or making new treasures for the room.

Basic Principles

The basic principles of my approach to decorating are very simple.

• **Buy or make only pieces that you absolutely love.** This is very important. The strongest thread running through every room should be your own personality and preferences. Whether or not you're consciously aware of the connections, pieces that speak to your heart and soul are always related to one another in some way.

• **Stick to your color palette.** If you haven't yet decided on a color palette, stop right here. Read pages 10 through 15 and select colors before you do another thing. These are not the only colors you will use, but they form an organizing principle that helps avoid visual chaos.

• **Balance sizes, scales, textures, and patterns.** To create balance, think in terms of opposites. If you choose an oversized piece, make a point of also selecting something more delicate. Deliberately mix large-, mid-, and small-scale patterns. If the room is filled with vertical lines, add some horizontal ones.

• **Leave white space.** Every room needs places for your eyes to rest.

The Fine Art of Scrounging

As you look through the projects and read the directions, you'll notice that we often begin with "salvaged" materials. This is a polite term. The truth is that Tim and I will use anything we can beg, borrow, or.... Well, we've never actually stolen anything, but we have pulled things out of Dumpsters and off curbs on trash days. (At least we always ask first.) We're both also incurable fans of estate and garage sales, flea markets, and junk stores. Here are some of the tricks we've developed for acquiring materials.

Start by looking through your own attic, basement, garage, or other storage areas where you might have stashed items that could be refurbished or adapted to other uses. It helps to look at old things with new eyes, trying to see not so much what they are as what they could be. When you've been through the nooks and crannies of your own home, branch out to the homes of family and friends. Tell people about your interest in old things and volunteer to help clean out storage areas any time you get the chance. You never know what might turn up in someone's attic or basement during spring cleaning or when they're packing to move.

If you see something you're interested in at a curb or in a Dumpster, don't be shy. I've never gotten over the need to ask first, but most people consider anything that has obviously been discarded as trash to be fair game. Either way, there are treasures to be had simply by keeping a sharp eye out and being brave.

Shop estate and garage sales, flea markets, junk stores, and salvage yards. Watch for annual neighborhood garage sales, which can offer lots of selection within one stop. Tim, who reads the classified ads each week, swears that the words "kids' clothes" are

the kiss of death. Families young enough to be recycling kids clothing must not be old enough to own the kind of junk we want. On the other hand, Tim says that words like "moving sale" or "40 years' accumulation" promise great possibilities.

When you go treasure hunting, be prepared.
- *Go grubby. Sellers often size up buyers by their clothes, shoes, and jewelry. Don't appear to be able or willing to pay top dollar.*
- *Bring cash in small denominations ($20 and smaller). It's almost always easier to get the best price if you're offering cash, and sellers don't always have change.*
- *Carry room drawings with dimensions and a tape measure. Bring your sketchbook and samples, too, but leave them in the car unless you really need to refer to them. (Prices skyrocket if you appear to be a decorator.)*
- *Drive the largest vehicle you can get access to and stock it with boxes or bags, padding, and string, rope, or bungee cords.*

At sales of all sorts, timing is everything. Go early and often. The early morning hours often are the time when dealers and professional pickers are combing the sales for the best pieces or trendiest merchandise. There's no way around it—if you want the best selection, you have to get there first. Although many people do it, we don't recommend knocking on doors before sales actually begin. A little consideration for others is in order, even when there are bargains at stake. For promising garage sales, make sure you're there at least fifteen minutes before the sale is scheduled to start. Here in the Midwest, people gather very early for estate sales. By custom, the first person in line hands out numbers to those who follow. In some cases there's a common agreement that people can go have coffee or a nap and then return to line in order of their original appearance. In other situations, it's understood that you have to be present to hold your place in line. If

ADD 2 INCHES

you're not sure about the procedure, ask someone who appears to be a regular. Believe me, bargain hunters can be fiercely protective, and you don't want to start the day with a disagreement over who gets the first look at the treasures.

Arriving early is a good strategy, but being there at the end of a sale has advantages as well. Occasionally, tired sellers who are more than ready to be finished are willing to bargain rather than repack their wares. Also, people who organize estate sales often make arrangements for a Dumpster to be delivered on sale day. When the sale closes, many things that didn't sell get tossed. If you're on hand when that process begins, you might find treasures free for the asking. If you offer to help, you're almost sure to be given the green light to take a few things that interest you. The same sort of idea works with garage sales. People often give their garage sale leftovers to charitable organizations. At the end of a sale, introduce yourself and offer to help organize or cart away whatever remains—you might strike gold.

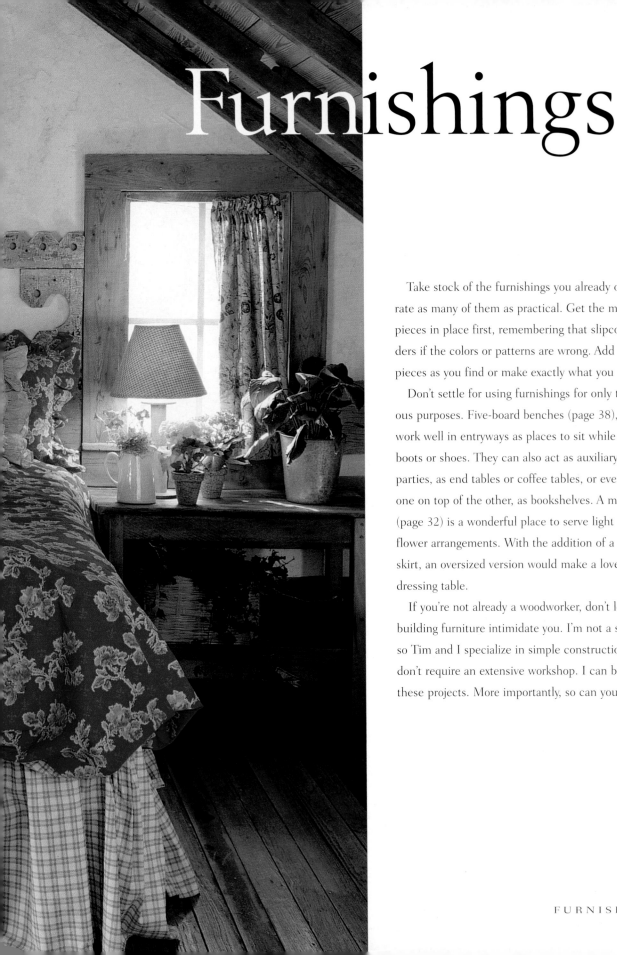

Furnishings

Take stock of the furnishings you already own and incorporate as many of them as practical. Get the major upholstered pieces in place first, remembering that slipcovers work wonders if the colors or patterns are wrong. Add non-upholstered pieces as you find or make exactly what you want and need.

Don't settle for using furnishings for only their most obvious purposes. Five-board benches (page 38), for example, work well in entryways as places to sit while changing out of boots or shoes. They can also act as auxiliary seating during parties, as end tables or coffee tables, or even, when stacked one on top of the other, as bookshelves. A mirrored tray table (page 32) is a wonderful place to serve light meals or display flower arrangements. With the addition of a simple fabric skirt, an oversized version would make a lovely vanity or dressing table.

If you're not already a woodworker, don't let the idea of building furniture intimidate you. I'm not a skilled craftsman, so Tim and I specialize in simple construction methods that don't require an extensive workshop. I can build every one of these projects. More importantly, so can you.

One of the major characteristics that separates cottages from small houses is a strong link to nature. Garden-themed furnishings celebrate that link and provide wonderful backgrounds for floral fabrics and interesting accessories. The picket-fence inspired banquette and chairs in the breakfast nook above offer an appropriate setting for the bunches of blooms on their cushions and pillows. In the sitting area at right, a park bench sets a tone that's reinforced by birdhouses, terra-cotta pots, and other gardening icons.

Paint is a great equalizer. Let's say you have a collection of inexpensive, casual furniture such as the pieces in the room at left. Left in their natural states, these pieces might have been a pretty rag-tag collection, but robed in white paint and set to sparkle against a yellow background, they present a unified front. The individual pieces in the sitting room above are more sophisticated, but the principle is the same. Green and white paint is mixed and matched with various fabrics to effortlessly blend a patchwork of styles and periods.

Working with all white furnishings is common in cottage style, and by and large it works well. If you decide to adopt that strategy, use either a broad palette of warm whites or include some strong color on the walls or in the fabrics and accents. Without that variety, all-white rooms begin to look cold and sterile—a bit like the inside of a refrigerator—rather than inviting and cozy.

GLASS-TOP TABLE

Add a flowing skirt and painted glass top to make a plain-Jane table into a star.

1 *Cut a circle of MDF sized to fit the base. (We used a 30" [762 mm] circle.) Prime and paint both sides of the MDF. When the paint is dry, mark the positions of the base's legs onto one side. Drill one hole through the center and another through one side of each end cap. Use ½" screws to attach the caps. Set the legs into the caps, insert a self-tapping screw into each, and tighten until the legs are stable.*

2 *Enlarge and photocopy the pattern on page 135. Set the glass tabletop on top of the pattern. Apply glass primer, to a small area of glass, then paint the design. When the first coat is dry, add a second. (Read and follow the paint manufacturer's specific directions.) Add four self-adhesive bumpers, then place the glass right side up on the table.*

3 *Measure from the table edge to the floor and add 5" (127 mm). Cut muslin to this length, enough pieces to equal 2½ times the table's circumference. Seam the pieces together, then make a narrow or rolled hem at one edge. Repeat with the chiffon. At the unhemmed edge, sew or serge the layers together, then turn down 2" (51 mm). Divide the skirt into quarters and mark them. Half an inch from the top edge, zigzag over a piece of dental floss. Start a new piece of floss at each quarter mark. For each quarter, pin one end of the floss and pull the other to gather the skirt. Adjust until the skirt fits around the table, distribute the gathers evenly and tie off the dental floss. Glue the gathered edge to the table. Add a decorative brass tack every three inches.*

MATERIALS:

• SALVAGED TABLE BASE • ½" (13 MM) COPPER END CAPS
• ½" (13 MM) DRYWALL SCREWS • ⅜" (10 MM) SELF-TAPPING SCREWS
(ONE PER LEG) • ¾" (19 MM) MDF • GLASS TABLE TOP • PRIMER &
PAINT • NO-HEAT GLASS PAINTS • GLASS PRIMER • SELF-ADHESIVE
BUMPERS • 6 YDS (5.5 MM) UNBLEACHED MUSLIN • 6 YDS (5.5 MM)
CHIFFON OR ORGANZA • DENTAL FLOSS • DECORATIVE BRASS TACKS

DECOUPAGE TABLETOP

Make any meal a special occasion with this whimsical decoupaged table.

1 From ¾" MDF, cut one 48"-diameter (1220 mm) round tabletop and a table anchor sized to match the arms of your pedestal base. Rout the edges of the tabletop with an ogee bit. Mark the center of the tabletop and of the anchor. Match those centers and attach the anchor to the table top, using 1½" screws driven down from the top. Fill the screw holes with lightweight spackle. When dry, lightly sand the spackle. Turn the tabletop over; mark and drill pilot holes on the anchor to match the arms of the pedestal base (as shown at right).

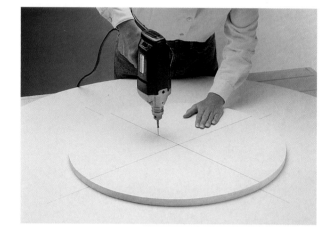

MATERIALS:

¾" (19 MM) MDF • 1½" (38 MM) WOOD SCREWS • LIGHTWEIGHT SPACKLE • PRIMER • LATEX PAINT, OFF WHITE • SPRAY GLOSS ENAMEL, GRAY OR TAUPE • LACE FABRIC OR TABLECLOTH • VINTAGE PLATES (4) • VINTAGE SILVERWARE (1 PLACE SETTING) • WHITE GLUE • WATER-BASED POLYURETHANE VARNISH • 2" (5 CM) WOOD SCREWS

2 Prime the tabletop and let it dry; add two coats of off-white paint. Smooth the lace over the top and tape it to the back. Spray an even coat of gray or taupe enamel over the lace, including the edges of the table. Remove the lace when the paint is dry.

3 Make color photocopies of four vintage plates, enlarging each to approximately 12¾" (325 mm). Make color copies of vintage silver—four each of a knife, dinner and dessert fork, and spoon—enlarging each piece by

approximately 25%. Lightly sand the back of each image, then use a pair of small, sharp scissors to cut out each one.

4 Arrange the images to resemble a table setting, and lightly sand the table in the areas where the images will be placed. Dilute 3 parts of white glue with one part of water and paint it on the back of each image. Gently smooth the paper with a bone press, making sure there are no creases or folds. When the glue is dry, apply five or six coats of water-based polyurethane varnish, letting each coat dry before applying the next. With each coat, alternate between horizontal and vertical brushstrokes. Sand lightly between coats, and remove any dust with tack cloth. Install the pedestal base by driving 2" screws up through the holes in the pedestal and into the anchor and tabletop.

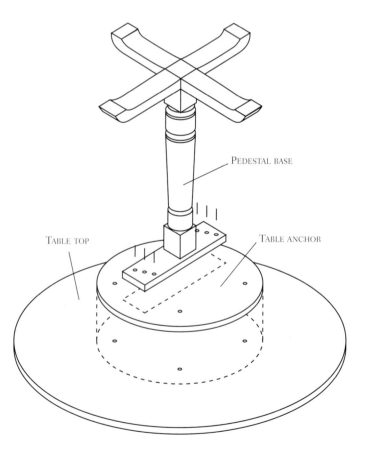

PEDESTAL BASE

TABLE TOP

TABLE ANCHOR

BASIC DECOUPAGE TECHNIQUES

To prepare the surface, sand the object until it's smooth, seal it with shellac or pigmented shellac, and let it dry. Lightly sand the coat of shellac and wipe away any dust with tack cloth. Apply two coats of paint and let them dry.

Cut out the images. Start by rough cutting with large scissors, then switch to small scissors to cut along the outside edges of the image. Hold the paper in one hand and turn it as you cut the curves.

Place the image on a cutting mat and use a craft knife to make delicate internal cuts.

Paint the backs of the images with slightly diluted white glue, and reposition them. Press the images down and

squeegee them with your fingers to remove any air bubbles or excess glue. Wipe away any excess glue with a damp cloth.

Apply coats of water-based varnish until you're satisfied with the surface. Between coats, let the varnish dry, then sand lightly. Just before adding the next coat of varnish, wipe the surface with tack cloth, taking care to remove all dust.

Apply stain with a paintbrush, then wipe away the excess with a soft, dry cloth, and let it dry. If desired, apply a coat of paste wax and polish the surface.

MIRRORED TRAY TABLE

Serve leisurely breakfasts or light snacks on this lovely tray table.

1 Remove the backing, glass, and all hanging hardware from the frame, then clean and lightly sand it. Center a handle on each end and mark the positions. Drill countersunk holes through the ends of the frame. Position the handles then insert and tighten the screws until the handles are stable. Fill the holes with wood filler and sand them lightly.

2 Measure the opening in the back of the frame and cut a piece of ¼" hardboard to fit. Place the hardboard on the frame and drill a countersunk pilot hole every 3 to 4" (76 to 100 mm). Drill a pilot hole near each corner as well as through the center of each candle cup.

3 Spray primer on the frame, backing, candle cups, and folding legs and let them dry. Add two coats of silver spray paint, allowing the paint to dry between coats. Working on one piece at a time, apply antiquing medium then wipe away the excess, using a clean, dry cloth. When the antiquing medium is dry, spray the pieces with sealer and let them dry. Position the mirror within the frame, add the backing, and screw the backing to the frame. Screw the candle cups to the corners of the backing. Rest the tray on the folding legs. (The candle cups will hold it in place.)

MATERIALS:

• SALVAGED FRAME, AT LEAST 12 × 24" (305 MM × 610 MM) • SALVAGED FOLDING LEGS OR LUGGAGE STAND • HANDLES (2) • LATEX WOOD FILLER • ¼" (6 MM) HARDBOARD • ¾" (19 MM) WOOD SCREWS • PRIMER • SILVER SPRAY PAINT • BLACK ANTIQUING MEDIUM • SEALER • MIRROR CUT TO FIT FRAME • WOOD CANDLE CUPS (4)

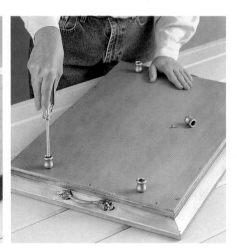

DROP LEAF TABLE

Borrow the ambience of vintage linens for a small table with big impact.

*1 Cut all pieces as indicted on the list below. Enlarge and photo-
copy the leaf pattern on page 132. Transfer the pattern to each 14 × 24"
piece of MDF. Use a jig saw to cut out the leaves.*

*2 Apply a coat of primer to both sides of the top, leaves, aprons,
and cleats, and let it dry. Add two coats of white paint, allowing the
paint to dry between coats. If it's necessary to prime and paint the legs,
do that now. When the paint is thoroughly dry, transfer the main pattern to each of the leaves (see page 125). Paint the design (see
Painting Tips on page 37). Add a ⅛" (3 mm) border of pink around the
shaped edges of the leaves and the ends of the table. (We used Delta
Ceramacoat's Hydrangea Pink, Wedgwood Green, Bungalow Blue, and
Mellow Yellow.)*

3 Make placement marks on the legs and both sides of the cleats as

Part	Material	Size	Number
Top	¾" MDF	19 × 24" (480 mm × 610 mm)	1
Leaf	¾" MDF	14 × 24" (350 mm × 610 mm)	2
Aprons & cleats	1 × 4	17" (430 mm)	4

MATERIALS:

• 8 FT. (2400 MM) CLEAR PINE 1 × 4 (19 × 89 MM) • ¾" (19 MM) MDF
• PRIMER • LATEX PAINT • CRAFT PAINT OR PAINT PENS • SALVAGED TABLE
LEGS (4) • #10 2½" (64 MM) WOOD SCREWS • 1¼" (32 MM) DRYWALL
SCREWS • TABLE HINGES (2 PAIRS) • DROP-LEAF SUPPORTS (1 PAIR)

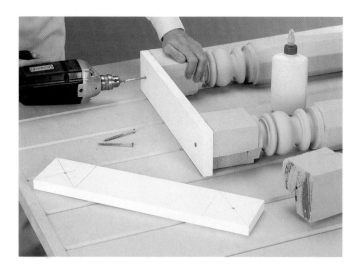

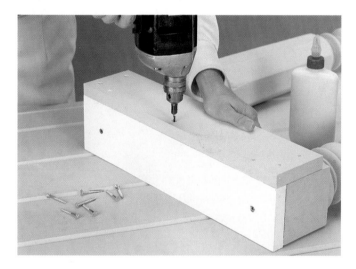

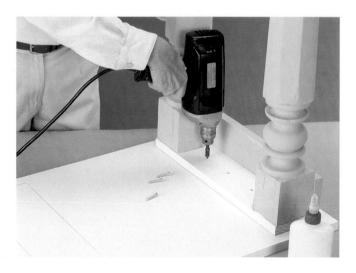

indicated in the diagram below. (Note: before gluing painted surfaces, use sandpaper to rough up the area to be glued.) Drill pilot holes at placement marks on cleats and legs. Spread wood glue over the tops of the legs. Align a cleat with the legs and attach it to each leg with a 2½" wood screw. Repeat with remaining cleat and pair of legs.

4 Place a cleat/leg assembly on the work surface and position the apron. Spread glue on the edge of the cleat and the face of the legs. Drill pilot holes and screw the apron to the cleat and to the center of each leg, using 1¼" drywall screws. Repeat with remaining cleat/leg assembly and apron.

5 Lay out and mark the cleat positions on the table top. Spread glue on the cleats, align them on the table, and drill pilot holes. Screw each cleat to the tabletop, using one 1¼" screw near each leg and one in the center.

6 Lay out the tabletop and one leaf on the work surface and use a combination square to mark the

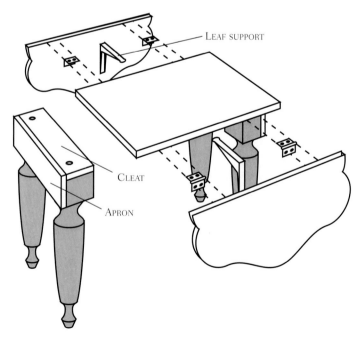

LEAF SUPPORT

CLEAT

APRON

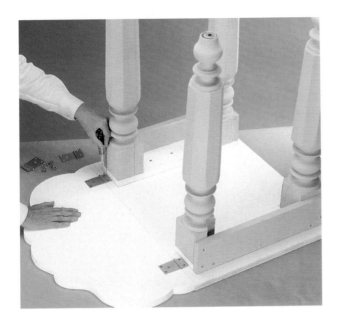
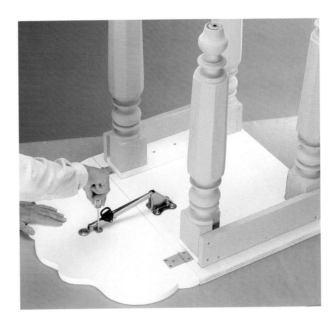

hinge positions. Drill pilot holes and attach the hinges to the leaves, using the screws supplied by the manufacturer. Double check the alignment of the pieces, then drill pilot holes and screw the hinges to the table-top. (We used brass plated table hinges from Rockler Woodworking and Hardware, part #29249.)

7 Position a drop leaf support between the cleats

and mark its position. Drill pilot holes, then attach the hardware to the table, using the screws provided by the manufacturer. (We used table drop leaf support #29637 from Rockler.) Follow the manufacturer's directions to level the leaf. Repeat steps 6 and 7 to add the remaining leaf to the opposite side of the table.

PAINTING TIPS:

The leaves of this table look like an embroidered dresser scarf, just like grandma used to make. The easiest way to imitate embroidery stitches is to use paint pens, but that limits your color selection. Painting with a brush is easy if you start with a good brush. My favorite is a #8 sable round point.

Wet your brush and load it with paint. Twirl the brush to form a point at the tip. Draw the point smoothly along the line.

For the loops that form the petals and leaves, leave a tiny space between the starting and end points. You can even add a tiny perpendicular line to the main "stitch," at the apex of the curve, to further imitate a lazy daisy stitch.

To make perfectly round, raised dots that look like French knots, dip the end of the paintbrush handle into the paint and touch it to the surface. Reload with paint after one or two dots.

FIVE-BOARD BENCH

Place this classic bench in front of a sofa, at the foot of a bed, or in a hallway.

1 Cut the parts as indicated on the list below. On each leg, mark the V and the notches as shown in the diagram on page 40. Use a jig saw to shape the legs. Also, make a mark 2" (50 mm) from the top and 2½" (65 mm) from the end on each end of the side pieces. Connect the marks, then cut along that line to shape the corners of the side pieces.

Part	Material	Length	Number
Side	1 × 6	42" (1070 mm)	2
Top	1 × 10	42" (1070 mm)	1
Legs	1 × 10	17" (430 mm)	2

MATERIALS:

• 8 FT. (2400 MM) 1 × 10 (19 × 254 MM) • 8 FT. 1 × 6 (12 × 140 MM)
• 1⅝" (42 MM) DRYWALL SCREWS • LATEX WOOD FILLER • WATER BASED STAIN
• SATIN-FINISH POLYURETHANE SEALER • LATEX PAINT (2 COLORS)
• DECORATIVE HANDLES (2)

2 On a level work surface, set one side piece into the notches on the legs. At each leg, drill countersunk pilot holes and then secure each joint with three drywall screws.

3 Set the top into position, its edge flush with the face of the side piece. Drill three countersunk pilot holes across the top and a hole about every 9" (230 mm) along the edge. Attach the top to the legs and side with drywall screws.

4 Turn the assembly upside down, and add the remaining side. (The edge of the side will be flush with the face of the top.) Drill three countersunk pilot holes down the

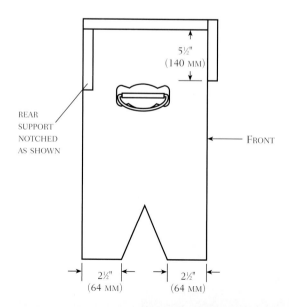

5½"
(140 MM)

REAR
SUPPORT
NOTCHED
AS SHOWN

FRONT

2½"
(64 MM)

2½"
(64 MM)

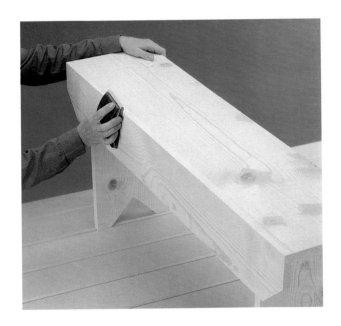

leg and a hole about every 9" along the edge. Drive drywall screws through the side and into the legs and top.

5 Fill all pilot holes with wood filler and allow them to dry. Lightly sand the entire bench, and remove the dust with a tack cloth. Apply a coat of stain to the bench and let it dry; add a coat of polyurethane sealer, and let that dry. Apply two coats of latex paint, a different color for each coat. Between coats, let the paint dry thoroughly, then lightly sand the bench, using fine-grit sandpaper. Wipe the bench with a tack cloth before applying the next coat. To reveal the layers of color, sand the bench with medium-grit sandpaper, sanding more thoroughly in some areas than others to remove layers unevenly. Avoid sanding beyond the stain.

6 Center a handle 5½" (140 mm) from the top of each leg. Drill pilot holes and drive screws to attach the handles to the bench.

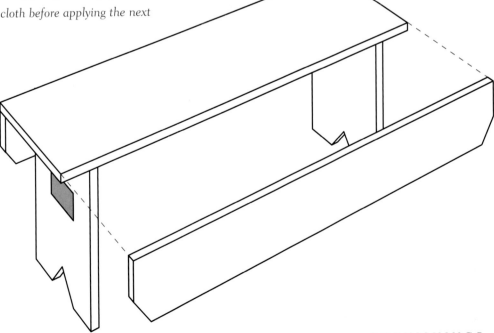

EMBELLISHED BOOKCASE

Give cottage character to a basic bookcase by adding interesting details.

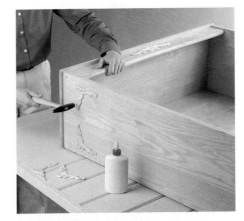

1 Sand the bookcase as necessary. Arrange the wood appliques and attach them according to the manufacturer's directions. (We drilled pilot holes and secured the appliques with wood glue and finish nails.) Prime the entire bookcase, inside and out, and let it dry. Paint the exterior and let it dry. Apply wallpaper sizing to the interior and let it dry, following the manufacturer's instructions. To give them more depth, paint the wood appliques with double strength coffee or tea.

2 Tear butcher paper into irregularly shaped pieces no larger than 6 × 6" (150 × 150 mm). Leave straight edges on some pieces for the top and bottom of the bookcase. Mix water and paint in a ratio of about 4:1. Wearing rubber gloves, dip a piece of paper into the paint mixture; hold it up and let most of the paint drip away. Gently crumple the paper, then flatten it on a plastic-covered surface and let it dry. Experiment with the amount that you crumple the paper and adjust the water to paint ratio until you get the effect you want. The paint will settle into the creases, so the more you crumple the paper, the more veins of color it will have.

3 Roll wallpaper adhesive onto both sides of a piece of prepared paper and paste it in place, smoothing the wrinkles outward from the center on each side with a wallpaper brush. Start with the straight-edged pieces at the top and bottom, then fill in the open areas with irregularly shaped pieces. Overlap the edges slightly; add pieces in alternating areas to allow each piece some time to dry before adding an overlapping piece. Smooth each piece to squeeze out any excess paste and remove any air bubbles. Rinse the brush as often as necessary to remove the excess paste. When the piece is completely dry, spray the interior with acrylic sealer.

Note: Practice by papering a scrap of foam core or plywood before working on the bookcase.

MATERIALS:

• SALVAGED BOOKCASE • DECORATIVE WOOD APPLIQUES • WOOD GLUE
• 4D (38 MM) FINISH NAILS • LATEX PRIMER • LATEX PAINT
• UNCOATED WHITE BUTCHER PAPER • WALLPAPER SIZING • WALLPAPER ADHESIVE
• SPRAY ACRYLIC SEALER

SIMPLE HEADBOARD

Build a simple headboard. Add sumptuous linens to make a restful place for body and soul.

1▸ Cut all parts listed below. Rout one edge of each piece of side and bottom trim, using a ⅜ × ½" (9.5 × 12.5 mm) piloted dado bit. On the front and back top trim pieces, make marks exactly 2" (50 mm) from each end. Starting and ending at these marks, rout the edge of each piece of top trim.

2▸ Lay out the top front trim with the dado facing up. Run a bead of wood glue along the dado, then fit the headboard base into position within the trim, precisely aligned with the 2" marks. Use pipe clamps to hold the trim in position against the base. Use a damp cloth to wipe away any excess glue, then let it dry.

3▸ Run a bead of glue along the dado on the back top trim, then clamp it in position on top of the base. Drill countersunk pilot holes and drive 1¼" drywall screws to secure the layers of trim. Again, wipe away any excess glue, and allow it to dry.

Part	Material	Size	Number
Base	Plywood	42 × 51" (1065 × 1295 mm)	1
Side Trim	1 × 3 poplar or clear pine	57⅜" (1455 mm)	4
Top Trim	1 × 3 poplar or clear pine	55" (1400 mm)	2
Bottom Trim	1 × 3 poplar or clear pine	52" (1320 mm)	2
Cap	1 × 3 poplar or clear pine	52" (1320 mm)	1

This headboard fits a full-size bed.

Note: When cutting trim pieces, especially front and back top trim, it's better to be slightly generous than short. If necessary, sand to fit.

MATERIALS:

4 × 8 FT. (1200 × 2400 MM) SHEET OF ¾" (19 MM) SOLID CORE VENEER PLYWOOD • 1 × 3 (19 × 65 MM) POPLAR OR PINE (30 FT. [10 M]) • 1¼" (32 MM) DRYWALL SCREWS • WOOD GLUE • 4D (38 MM) FINISH NAILS • WOOD APPLIQUE • LATEX WOOD FILLER • PAINT • ANTIQUING GLAZE • VARNISH • FURNITURE SLIDES (4) • HOLLYWOOD BED FRAME

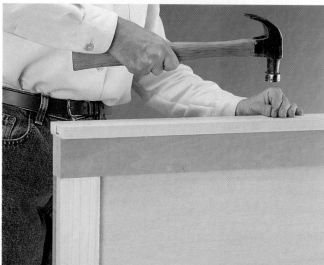

4 Repeat steps 2 and 3 with the back and front side trim, positioning the outside edges of the side trim flush with the ends of the top trim. At the bottom of the headboard, measure the opening between the side trim, then cut the front and back bottom trim to fit. Glue the front bottom trim in place and let it dry, then add the back bottom trim and screw the layers together as described in step 3.

5 Set the assembly right side up and run a generous bead of glue along the top edge of the upper trim. Center the cap on this top edge, overlapping the edges by ½" (12 mm). Tack the cap in place with 4d finish nails and let the glue dry.

6 Position the wood applique and mark placement lines on the face of the headboard. Drill pilot holes in the applique, then spread wood glue on the back. Apply the applique, then tack it in place with 4d finish nails. Let the adhesive dry.

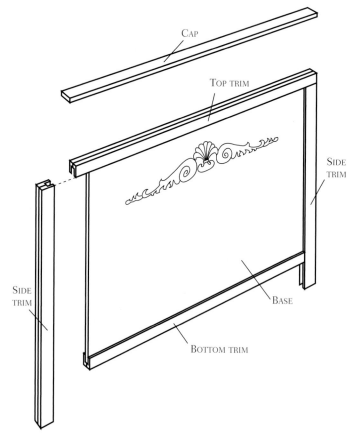

CAP

TOP TRIM

SIDE TRIM

SIDE TRIM

BASE

BOTTOM TRIM

7 *Fill all holes with wood filler, lightly sand the entire headboard, then clean the surface with a tack cloth. Apply two coats of ivory paint, allowing the paint to dry between coats.*

8 *Working on one manageable area at a time, apply a coat of antiquing glaze. (We used Ralph Lauren's Aging Glaze in Tea Stain.) Brush with the grain of the wood. While the glaze is still wet, use a slightly damp rag to wipe off the excess, wiping perpendicular to the grain. Use a cotton swab to remove excess glaze in the crevices of the applique. (Don't remove too much—the crevices in most old pieces are discolored by trapped dust.)*

9 *When the glaze is dry, apply two coats of varnish and let it dry. Tack a furniture slide to the bottom of each leg. Mark and drill holes in each leg, then use bolts to attach a Hollywood bed frame to the headboard.*

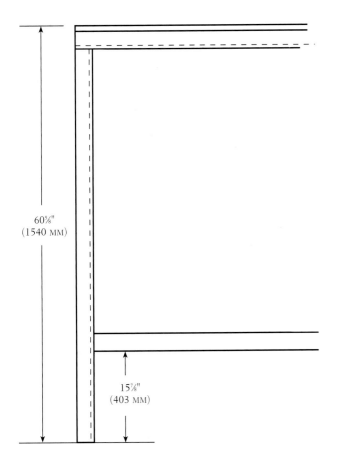

60⅝"
(1540 MM)

15⅞"
(403 MM)

Pillows & Linens

Pillows offer perfect opportunities to mix patterns and colors and textures. They also create the sense of comfort and luxury that's essential to cottage style. The script pillow on page 59 even lets you say what's on your mind. Make a bunch. Almost any room can be improved with pillows.

The degree of luxury provided by fine linens absolutely defies description. It isn't just that they feel good against your skin—which they do. It's more about how they make you feel inside: Pampered. Comforted. Optimistic. The only real downside to this luxury is that it often comes with a hefty price tag. Still, having at least one set of special linens for each bed in the house is a good investment. Buy plain, high quality linens and add lace and ribbons to give them a designer appearance without the designer's price (page 64).

Don't reserve your fine linens only for guests, though. When someone in the family is returning from an extended trip or even just a tough day, surprise them by making up their bed with freshly scented sheets and pillowcases. Before I leave on a trip, I make up my bed with my favorite sheets and blankets. If I'm not crazed the day before I go, I even press the pillowcases with scented ironing water. Don't laugh until you've tried falling into bed after an exhausting travel day, greeted by those fresh smells and soft textures. It feels wonderful and practically guarantees a good night's sleep.

Whether they're monochromatic like the white pillows above or wildly colorful like the 40's prints at right, vintage linens and reproduction fabrics make fabulous pillows for a cottage-style home. The key is to collect pillows in a wide variety of shapes and sizes. Create a foundation with big European squares, then layer on squares, rectangles, and bolsters to your heart's content. Add trims and fringe and ribbons and ruffles. Even buttons. Truly, the sky's the limit when it comes to imaginative pillows.

Great pillows can be extremely expensive to purchase or even to make. If you like the look of vintage linens but not the typical prices, buy damaged or stained pieces at bargain prices. You might be surprised at how often stains can be removed by rubbing them with a thick paste of salt and vinegar followed by a vinegar rinse and an hour or two in the sun. Some of the new oxygen bleach products work wonders, too. If all else fails, cut around the stains or cover them with ribbon or trim.

In cottage-style homes pillows are stacked on the floor, heaped on sofas, chairs, and benches, and arranged in abundant drifts on beds. Pillows make any space comfortable, cozy, and inviting; they bring color and a sense of luxury into almost any room.

The colorful floor pillows above are made from pillow ticking, tablecloths, and drapery fabrics. All are durable enough to be used every day. The more real use you expect a pillow to receive, the fewer trims and ruffles it should have. The knife edge pillows above would be terrific support for someone sitting on the floor to watch television, have a snack, or play games.

The bright pillows in the sitting room at left could be made from coordinated linen napkins. Napkins actually make great pillows. They're inexpensive, readily available, washable, and durable. Plus, in essence, they're precut and ready to sew into basic square pillow covers.

Pillows

Splash color into your rooms with one-of-a-kind pillows.

ENVELOPE PILLOW

MATERIALS:

- 1¼ YDS (1145 MM) SILK DUPIONI
- 1¼ YDS. SILK ORGANZA • 16" (410 MM) PIL-
LOW FORM • BUTTON (1)

1 Cut one 38½ × 17" (977 × 432 mm) and one 9 × 17" (229 × 432 mm) piece of dupioni; cut one 38½ × 17" piece of silk organza. Layer the 38½ × 17" organza rectangle over the silk one, then finish one 17" edge, using a zigzag stitch. At this edge, press 6" (153 mm) of the combined fabrics to the wrong side.

2 At the opposite (unfinished) end, stitch the assembly to the 9 × 17" rectangle, using a ½" (12 mm) seam. Finish the seam and press it toward the larger rectangle. Fold the long edge of the small rectangle in half, right sides together; stitch a ½" seam (see diagram). Clip the folded corner; press the seam open, then turn it to create

the folded point. Finish the edge, then turn to the right side and stitch in the ditch of the previous seam to secure the flap. Fold and press the flap along the seam.

3 With the flap folded down, fold the rectangle in half, right sides together, aligning the folds. Turn the 6" inner flap over the triangular flap. Stitch ½" seams on both sides of the rectangle. Turn the pillow cover right side out. At the point, mark and make a buttonhole.

4 Mark the button placement through the buttonhole, then add a button. Insert the pillow form, tuck it under the inner flap, and button the flap into position.

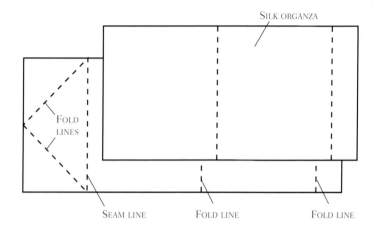

SILK ORGANZA

FOLD
LINES

SEAM LINE   FOLD LINE   FOLD LINE

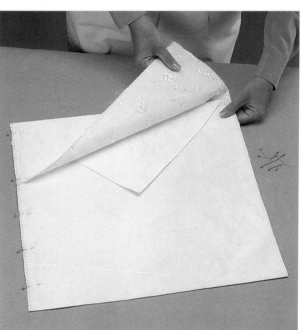

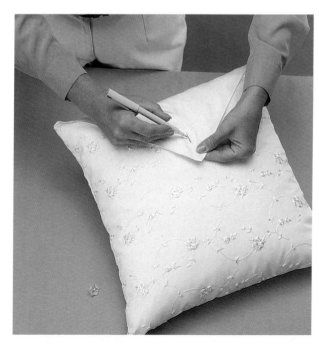

SILK FLOWER BOUQUET PILLOW

1 Cut two squares of fabric, each 1" (25 mm) larger than the pillow form. For example, we cut 15" squares to fit our 14" pillow form. Layer the squares, right sides together, and pin all four edges. In the center of one side, leave a 7" (180 mm) opening. Sew the layers together, leaving the unpinned portion open. Press the seams open, including the seam allowance of the opening. Turn the pillow cover right side out. (See page 123 for further information on pillows.)

2 Insert the pillow form into the cover. Clip away the stems of the silk flower assortment. Experiment until you've create a pleasing arrangement, then pin the flowers to the pillow cover. Remove the pillow form, then reach inside the cover and tack the flowers in place, using a few small stitches for each flower. Replace the form, then pin and slipstitch the opening.

MATERIALS:
• SILK DUPIONI • ASSORTMENT OF SILK FLOWERS • PILLOW FORM

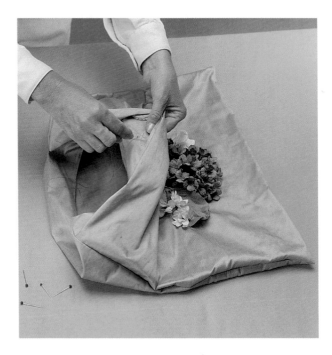

BASKET LINER PILLOW

MATERIALS:
* PILLOW FORM • LINEN BREADBASKET LINER • ½ YD.(460 MM) OF
COORDINATING FABRIC • BUTTONS (4)

1 *Select a pillow form that suits the size of your linen piece. (We used a 10" [255 mm] form.) Cut two squares of fabric, 1" (25 mm) larger than the pillow form. For example, we cut 11" (280 mm) squares to fit our 10" pillow form. (Be sure to center the pattern of the fabric.) Layer the squares, right sides together, and pin all four edges. In the center of one side, leave a 7" (180 mm) opening unpinned. Sew the layers together, leaving the unpinned portion open. Press the seams open, including the seam allowance of the opening. (See page 123 for more information on pillow construction.)*

2 *Turn the pillow cover right side out, insert the pillow form, and pin the opening. Slipstitch the opening. Arrange the liner around the finished pillow and pin it in place. Use a fabric marking pen to mark a buttonhole location near each point of the liner. Make the buttonholes as marked.*

3 *Repin the liner to the pillow. Reach through the button-holes to mark the button locations onto the pillow. Sew the buttons on as marked, then button the liner to the pillow.*

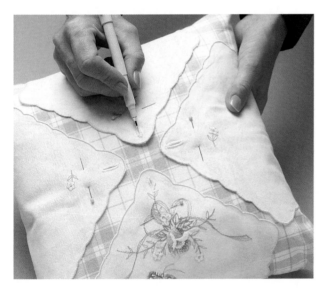

SCRIPT PILLOW

MATERIALS:

• 12 × 16" (305 × 410 MM) PILLOW FORM • ½ YARD (450 MM) OF FABRIC
• ASSORTMENT OF YARNS AND RIBBONS • HAIRPIN LACE LOOM
• SEAM TAPE

1 Photocopy the pattern on page 132. Cut two pieces of fabric, each 13 × 17" 335 × 435 mm). Set the photocopied pattern onto the right side of one of the pieces of fabric and press it with an iron to transfer the pattern. Place the end of the ribbon yarn at the beginning of the first letter, and bar tack the end. Sew the yarn to the pillow front, using a narrow zigzag stitch and following the lines of the pattern.

2 Layer together several pieces of ribbon yarn, tiny satin ribbon, fluffy yarn, including the ribbon yarn used for the script. Wrap the yarns and ribbons around the first 8" (200 mm) of a hairpin lace loom.

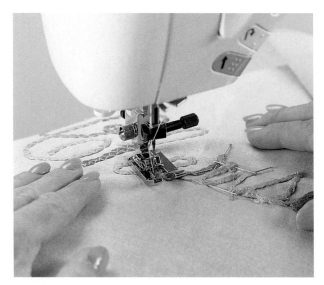

3 Lay a strip of seam tape at the center of the wrapped yarns, and stitch down its center, using a straight stitch. Slide this stitched portion off one end of the loom, and wrap another section of trim. Continue wrapping and stitching until you've created 57" (1450 mm) of trim. Fold the seam tape in half, which will double up the layers.

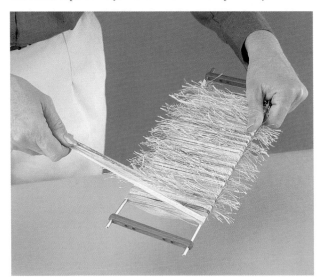

4 Mark a line around the perimeter of the pillow front, ½" (12 mm) from the edge. Aligning the folded edge of the seam tape with the marked line, pin the trim around the pillow top; baste the trim in place. Add the pillow back, right sides together, and pin; leave a 7" (180 mm) opening unpinned. Sew the layers together, leaving the unpinned portion open. Press the seams open, then turn the pillow cover right side out. Insert the form, pin and slipstitch the opening. (See page 125 for additional information.)

Note: To make your own word patterns, choose a font and type the words. Select "Flip Horizontal" in the "Style" menu to create a mirror image. Print the pattern, enlarge it on a photocopier if necessary, and proceed.

PIECED PILLOW

MATERIALS:

EMBROIDERED VINTAGE LINEN • DECORATOR FABRIC FOR INNER BORDER, CORNER TRIANGLES, OUTER BORDER AND BACK • GIMP TRIM • COORDINATING FRINGE • PILLOW FORM

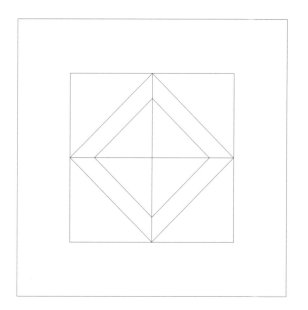

1 To make a plan for your pillow, first decide on the finished pillow size. Next, evaluate the embroidered piece and decide on the dimensions of the insert. Remember that the embroidery should be centered "on point" within a square. Make a tissue paper pattern the size of the finished pillow (see diagram). Divide the square into quarters, then draw the insert square at the center. Starting and ending at the quarter marks, add inner borders and corner triangles. Draw individual pattern pieces, adding ¼" (6 mm) seam allowances to the insert, inner border, and corner triangle patterns. Add a total of ¾" (19 mm) for seam allowances to the outer

borders. Do not add a seam allowance to the base. Cut the pieces. (We cut an 11" (280 mm) base; a 6" (155 mm) insert; two 1⅝ × 6" (42 × 155 mm) and two 1⅝ × 8¼" (42 × 210 mm) inner borders; four 6¼ × 6¼ × 9" (160 × 160 × 230 mm) corner triangles; two 4¼ × 11½ (108 × 292 mm) and two 4¼ × 19" (108 × 485 mm) outer borders.)

2 Make ¼" seams unless otherwise noted. Sew the shorter inner borders to opposite sides of the insert. Sew the longer inner borders to remaining sides. Sew a corner triangle to each side of the assembly. Press the seams away from the insert. Layer the right side of the base to the wrong side of the square; sew a shorter border to the top and bottom, then add a longer border to each side.

3 Position gimp across the pillow front at the seams for the top and bottom borders. Stitch the gimp in place with a medium zigzag stitch. Repeat at the side borders. Using the pillow front as a pattern, cut the pillow back.

4 Machine baste the fringe to the right side of the pillow front so the heading of the trim is even with the edges. At each end, cut the fringe between two loops and handstitch the last loop to secure it; butt the ends of the fringe together. Pin the pillow front to the back, rights sides together. Stitch a ½" (12 mm) seam around the pillow cover, leaving an opening on one side; press the seam open. Trim the corners diagonally and turn the pillow cover right side out. Insert the pillow form and slipstitch the opening. (See page 125 for more information.)

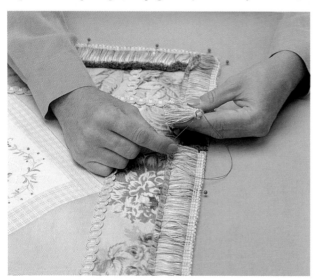

FLEECE BLANKET

Combine an old-fashioned design and a modern fabric to produce this unique coverlet.

1 *Cut a 72 × 60" (1.83 × 1.52 m) piece of cream fleece. Cut off the selvage edges, and round off the corners. Cut ¾"-wide (19 mm) strips of fleece: about 18 strips of cream, 6 pink, 4 green, and 3 blue. Stretch each strip: Grasp the end firmly with one hand and pull the fabric between the thumb and forefinger of your other hand. As it's stretched, the fleece will curl and develop a chenille-like appearance.*

2 *Enlarge the pattern on page 131, then mark the design onto the blanket (see page 125). Using an open-toe applique foot and a medium zigzag stitch, sew a cream strip to each straight line. Lay the strip on top of the line and feed it under the foot without creating any tension. Bar tack at each end. Starting at the center of each flower, sew strips to form the petals, then add the centers. Finally, form the leaves and stems. Again, bar tack at each end.*

3 *At the outside edges of the blanket, fold ⅜" (9 mm) to the wrong side and pin it in place. Stitch the hem in place, using a twin needle.*

MATERIALS:

- 2⅛ YARDS (1.94 M) CREAM SYNTHETIC FLEECE, 60" (1.52 M) WIDE
- ½ YARD (460 MM) EACH, PINK, BLUE AND GREEN SYNTHETIC FLEECE

EMBELLISHED LINENS

Treat yourself or your guests to luxurious lace-trimmed sheets and pillowcases.

SHEET FLAP

Sheet size	2" Lace & Ribbon	½" Lace
Twin	2 yds (1 m) each	8 yds (7.3 m)
Full	2⅓ yds (2 m) each	9⅓ yds (8.5 m)
Queen	2⅝ yds (2.4 m) each	10½ yds (9.6 m)
King	3⅛ yds (2 m) each	12½ yds (11.4 m)

MATERIALS:
• 2 FLAT SHEETS • LACE TRIM, ABOUT 2" (5 CM) WIDE • FLAT LACE
TRIM, ½ TO 1" (1.3 TO 2.5 CM) WIDE • DECORATIVE RIBBON • BUTTONS

This bedding was created by our enormously talented sample artist and friend, Sheila Duffy.

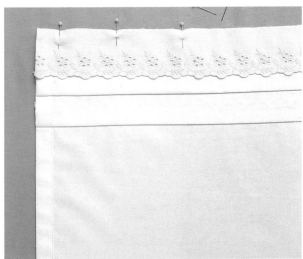

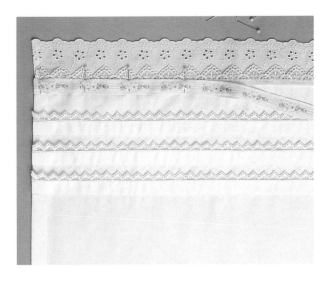

1 Cut a 24¾" (630 mm) strip from the upper edge of one of the sheets. Place the fabric with the right side down and the raw edge to the top, on an ironing surface. Turn down the first 10" (255 mm), and press a fold. Press a second fold 7" (180 mm) from the raw edge, taking care not to press out the fold of the first tuck. Press a third fold 4" (105 mm) from the raw edge. To make the tucks, stitch ¾" (19 mm) from the edge of each fold. Press the tucks toward the raw edge, then press 1¼" (32 mm) of the raw edge to the wrong side.

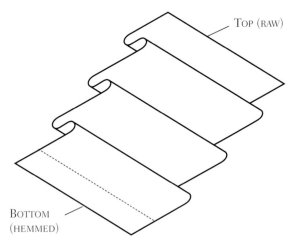

TOP (RAW)

BOTTOM
(HEMMED)

2 Insert narrow lace trim under each fold, and stitch close to the folded edge, securing the lace. Pin the 2" lace to the raw edge, wrong sides together, with the ends of the trim extending ½" (12 mm) beyond the side edges. Fold the ends of the trim under ¼" (6 mm) twice to the wrong side. Stitch ¼" from the raw edge of the fabric. Press the seam toward the fabric. Hand or machine-stitch hems at the ends of the trim.

3 Lap the pressed edge over the seam allowance on the right side, encasing it; extend the pressed edge about ⅛" (3 mm) over the previous stitching. Center decorative ribbon over the last flap; pin ribbon in place. Stitch close to the folded edge, inserting narrower lace trim under the fold. Topstitch ⅝" (16 mm) from the edge of the lace, stitching through all layers.

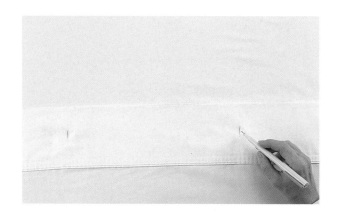

4 *Make placement marks for buttonholes on the upper hemmed edge of the second top sheet, centering the buttonholes on the hem and spacing them about 12" (305 mm) apart. Stitch the buttonholes. Align the top sheet and the sheet flap, wrong sides together, overlapping the hemmed edges. Mark corresponding placement for the buttons. On the wrong side of the decorative sheet flap, stitch a button to each mark. Button the decorative sheet flap onto the top sheet.*

PILLOWCASES

Pillow Size	Fabric	2" Lace & Ribbon	½" Lace
Standard	40½ × 32" (1030 × 81 mm)	1¼ yd (1.1 m) each	3¾ yd (3.3 m)
Queen	40½ × 36" (1030 × 915 mm)	"	"
King	40½ × 42"(1030 × 1070 mm)	"	"

1 *Cut two pillowcases from the remainder of the cut sheet. For the first pillowcase, press a foldline 7" and 4" (180 and 105 mm) from the 40½" edge of fabric. Stitch tucks and attach trim as in steps 2 through 4 above. Cut the ends of the trim even with the edge of the fabric.*

2 *Fold the fabric in half, right sides together, matching raw edges. Stitch ¼" from the raw edges. Finish the seams, using a zigzag or overlock stitch. Turn the pillowcase right side out. Repeat with remaining pillowcase.*

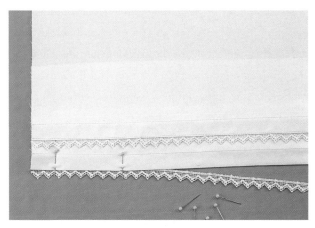

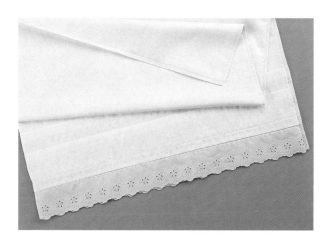

SCALLOPED BLANKET

MATERIALS:
• POLAR FLEECE • COORDINATING THREAD • QUILTING TEMPLATE
• 2.0 TWIN NEEDLE

1 Determine the finished length and width of the blanket, and calculate how much fabric you need (see page 69 for further details and page 130 for a diagram). Cut the center panel and both borders of the blanket. Lay out the center panel and use a washable fabric marker to draw lines 17½" (445 mm) from the bottom and 6½" (165 mm) from each side. Experiment with the quilting template you've selected; arrange a pleasing number of repeats along the sides and end of the blanket. Mark the template onto the back of the fabric. Using a twin needle and a 2.25" stitch length (and working from the back), stitch over each marked line.

2 Sew a border to each side of the center panel. Pin the seam open, then use a twin needle to stitch it down.

3 Cut a 58½ × 8½" (1485 × 215 mm) strip of fleece and two 11¼ × 8½ strips. Sew one small strip to each end of the larger strip; fold the resulting strip in half, wrong sides together. Pin the folded strip to the right side of the upper edge of the blanket, and stitch the two together, using a ¼" (6 mm) seam. Finger press the seam toward the center of the blanket, then stitch down it from the back, using a twin needle.

4 Working with the quilting template, calculate an even number of scallops along the sides and across the end of the blanket. Mark the scallops onto the back of the fabric and cut them out. Cut around the curves with a rotary cutter, then clip into the points with a pair of small scissors.

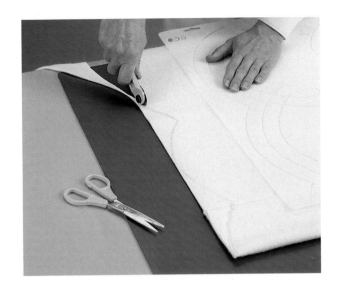

TO MEASURE THE BLANKET:

Make the bed with the linens that will normally be on it. Measure the length of the bed from the head to the foot (a). Measure the width of the bed from side to side (b). Measure the drop length (c) from the top of the mattress to the desired finished length, 1 to 4" (25 to 100 mm) below the top of the box spring.

To calculate the amount of fabric necessary:
Find the number of widths by dividing the cut width of the blanket by the fabric width: round off to the next highest number. Multiply the number of widths by the cut length to determine the amount of fabric needed.

To cut the pieces:
Cut the center panel to equal B + 4" × A + C minus 4" (the width of the bed plus 2" on each side by the length of the bed plus the drop length minus a few inches clearance at the top of the bed). Cut two borders to equal C minus 2" × A + C

minus 4" (the drop length minus 2" by the length of the bed plus the drop length minus 4"). For example, for our full-sized bed, we cut our center panel 58½ x 80¼" (1490 × 2040 mm), two side borders 11¼ x 80¼" (290 × 2040 mm), an upper center border, 8½ × 58½" (220 × 1490 mm), and two upper side borders 8½ × 11¼" (220 × 290 mm).

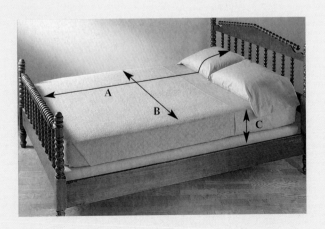

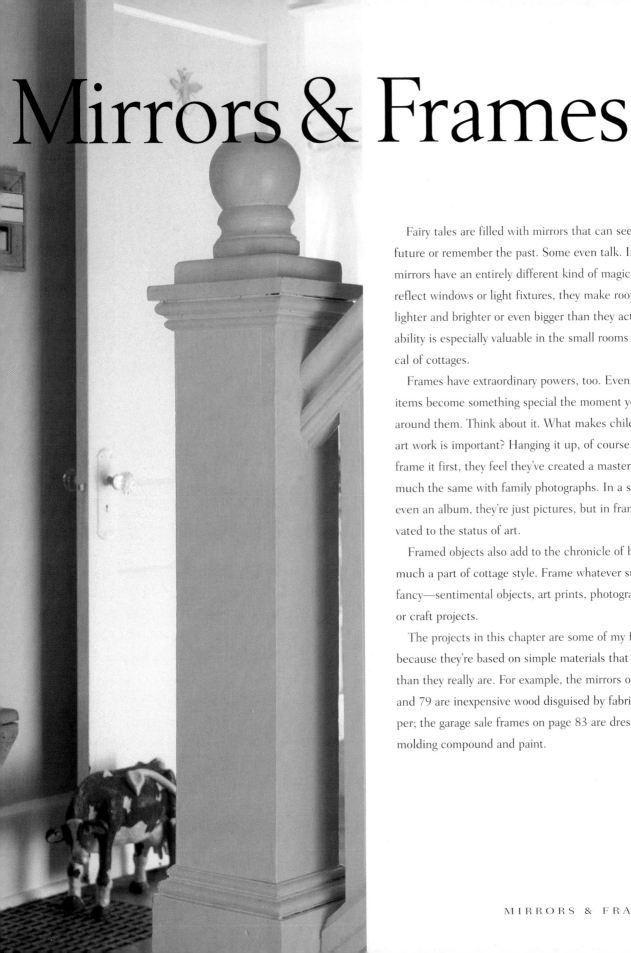

Mirrors & Frames

Fairy tales are filled with mirrors that can see into the future or remember the past. Some even talk. In real life, mirrors have an entirely different kind of magic. Placed to reflect windows or light fixtures, they make rooms appear lighter and brighter or even bigger than they actually are. This ability is especially valuable in the small rooms that are typical of cottages.

Frames have extraordinary powers, too. Even ordinary items become something special the moment you put a frame around them. Think about it. What makes children feel their art work is important? Hanging it up, of course. And if you frame it first, they feel they've created a masterpiece. It's much the same with family photographs. In a shoebox or even an album, they're just pictures, but in frames they're elevated to the status of art.

Framed objects also add to the chronicle of history that's so much a part of cottage style. Frame whatever suits your fancy—sentimental objects, art prints, photographs, artwork or craft projects.

The projects in this chapter are some of my favorites because they're based on simple materials that look like more than they really are. For example, the mirrors on pages 78 and 79 are inexpensive wood disguised by fabric and wallpaper; the garage sale frames on page 83 are dressed up with molding compound and paint.

Mirrors stretch the boundaries of the small bathroom at right. Even one well placed mirror multiplies light and space, but collections have a special charm. They work best when the frames are relatively the same style, color, and size, but have enough variation among them to make the display interesting. Here the distressed painted finish of the accent wall is repeated in frames of the same approximate size but differing shapes.

Mirrors don't always have to be hung on walls. Try adding them to tabletop displays, for example. The elaborate white frames of the mirrors on the bedside table above were chosen to complement the lace of the dresser scarf. Even though they're small, these mirrors are positioned to reflect several accessories, adding an extra bit of color and sparkle to the room.

If you haven't had much practice arranging displays, relax. This is fun. Arranging mirrors or any other group of accessories is something like composing a still life. The space you're accessorizing acts as the background and the goal is to create balance between the objects and the background.

Lay out the collection on the floor or a table so that you can study the sizes and shapes of the items. Play with the pieces until something speaks to you as a starting point. The largest pieces act as anchors for the rest of the collection, so it often makes sense to start with those.

Don't crowd the arrangement; let open spaces lead the eye around the image you're creating. Use an uneven number of pieces and avoid perfect symmetry. When you stagger two objects, place the top of one about a third of the way down from the top of the other.

Few accessories are more important to cottage-style homes than framed photographs. Frame your favorites and place them in groupings throughout the house. The frames of each grouping can match if you insist, but I prefer frames that have complementary colors and shapes that look as though they belong together rather than actually matching. The framed photos on the corner shelf in the bedroom at left appear to represent cherished childhood memories. The differences in the frames reinforce the impression that they were collected over time.

Try grouping photos by the era in which they were taken. This approach lets you match the style of the frames to the images. For example, the tortoise shell look of the frames in the grouping above is especially suited to the sepia-toned photographs they display. In my own home, the family room mantle is crowded with gold framed portraits of my children. A skirted table in the living room shows off silver-framed photos of my beloved grandparents and great-grandparents. A shelf in my bedroom carries colorfully framed reminders of my children as toddlers—photos as well as several very early art projects.

Mirrors

Reflect your good taste with unique, easy-to-make mirrors.

MOSAIC MIRROR

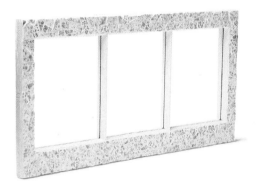

MATERIALS:

• SALVAGED WINDOW SASH • SAFETY GLASSES • HEAVY GLOVES
• DISHES OR TILES • TILE MASTIC • GROUT • CUSTOM-CUT MIRROR
• ⅛" (3 MM) HARDBOARD • GLAZING POINTS • EYE SCREWS AND PICTURE WIRE

Note: Choose a horizontal sash divided by mullions. Choose dishes with at least three colors in patterns that can be blended evenly.

◢ *1* Remove any hardware from the sash. Wearing heavy gloves, run a razor knife between the glass and sash, then remove the glass and glazing. Clean and lightly sand the sash. Put the

dishes or tiles in a heavy paper bag and use a rubber mallet to break them. (Wear safety glasses.) Arrange the mosaic pieces on the work surface around the outside edges of the sash. If necessary, use tile nippers to refine pieces to fit. Spread an even coat of mastic over the first 12" (300 mm) of the interior side of the sash. Transfer the mosaic to the sash. Continue working on about 12" at a time. As the mosaic on each side is completed, make any necessary adjustments then press each piece into the mastic to create an even, flat finish. Let the mastic dry overnight. Grout the mosaic and use a damp sponge to wipe away the excess. When the grout has dried slightly, polish away the remaining grout film, using a soft cloth.

◁2▷ Cut a piece of ⅛" hardboard to fit each opening.

Insert a piece of mirror and a piece of hardboard into each opening and push glazing points into the sash to retain them. Install eye screws and hanging wire.

FABRIC-COVERED MIRROR

MATERIALS:

- 8 FT. (2400 MM) PINE 1 × 6 (19 × 140 MM) (1) • 1 YD. (915 MM) OF INSULATED DRAPERY LINING • 88" (2100 MM) OF BORDER FABRIC • WOOD GLUE • POLYURETHANE GLUE • 1" (25 MM) DRYWALL SCREWS • 10" (255 MM) SQUARE MIRROR • HANGING HARDWARE AND WIRE • ¼" (7 MM) PLYWOOD

◁1▷ Cut a 19½" (480 mm) square of ¼" plywood and set it aside. For the frame, cut four 20" (500 mm) pieces of 1 × 6, mitering the ends of each piece at opposing 45° angles. Using a ¼" (6 mm) straight bit, rout the inside edge of the back of each frame piece. Cut four 5½ × 20" (140 × 500 mm) pieces of insulated drapery lining, and four 7 × 24" (180 × 600 mm) pieces of border fabric. Spread a thin layer of wood glue across the top of each piece of the frame.

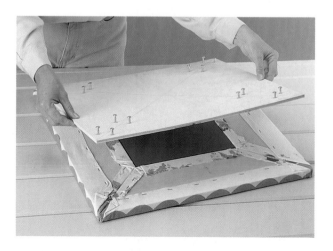

Smooth a piece of lining on top of each, and let the glue dry. If necessary, trim the lining flush with the edges.

2 Lay each board, lining side down, on the wrong side of a piece of fabric. Starting at the angled ends, wrap the fabric to the back of the board and staple it in place.

3 Spread polyurethane glue on the ends of each wrapped board, assemble the frame, and secure it with a strap clamp. When the glue is dry, set the mirror in place. Mark the joint locations on the plywood backing, then start two screws on each

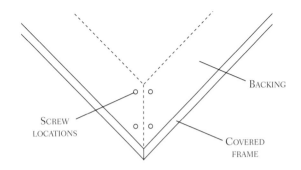

side of each joint. Position the backing and drive the screws into the frame to secure the joints. Add hanging hardware.

TEXTURED MIRROR

1 Mark and cut out a 27 × 22" (690 × 560 mm) oval from ½" MDF (see page 126). Mark a 17¾ × 14¼" (450 × 360 mm) oval at the center, then drill a ¼" (6 mm) hole along the marked line. Slip the blade of a jig saw into the hole and cut out the interior oval. For the backing, cut a 20 × 16¼" (510 × 410 mm) piece of ½" MDF, then cut an 18 × 14¼" (460 × 360 mm) oval from the center. Using a ¼" straight bit, rout the edge of the oval.

2 Cut two 9"-wide (230 mm) half-ovals of wallpaper. Carefully clip the inside and outside edges at 1" (25 mm) intervals. Paper the frame, wrapping the edges. (Follow the manufacturer's instructions regarding wetting and booking the paper.) Paint the frame. (We used Delta Ceramacoat's Wedgwood Green and a brown antiquing glaze.)

3 Set the mirror on the back of the frame, add the backing, and screw the layers together. Tap in a decorative upholstery

MATERIALS:
• ½" (12 MM) MDF • PAINTABLE, TEXTURED WALLPAPER • LATEX PAINT
• CUSTOM-CUT MIRROR • 1" (25 MM) WALLBOARD SCREWS
• SCREW EYES AND PICTURE WIRE • DECORATIVE UPHOLSTERY TACKS

tack every 3" (75 mm) around the perimeter of the frame. Add screw eyes and hanging wire.

Frames

Display favorite photos or prints in fabulous frames.

BEADBOARD FRAME

MATERIALS:

BEADBOARD • ¼" HARDBOARD • BRADS • WOOD GLUE • PRIMER • LATEX PAINT
• 7 × 13½" GLASS • RETAINER CLIPS • HANGING HARDWARE AND WIRE

1 *Cut a piece of beadboard, 10 × 17" (255 × 435 mm). On the back of the beadboard, mark three 3 × 5" (75 × 125 mm) rectangles, centered on the beadboard and 2" (50 mm) apart from one another. Drill a small hole in one corner of each marked rectangle. For each, slip the blade of a jig saw into the hole, and cut along the marked lines. If necessary, use a straightedge and a utility knife to clean up the cuts.*

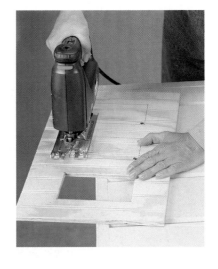

2 Cut a 9 × 15½" (230 × 395 mm) piece of hardboard, then cut a 7 × 13½" (205 × 355 mm) piece from the middle, leaving a 1"-wide (25 mm) rectangle. Center this on the back of the frame; glue and tack it in place. Prime and paint the frame and let it dry. Set the glass in place. Tape the photos or prints to a 7 × 13½" piece of hardboard. Set the backing into the frame and attach four retainer clips to hold it in place. Add hanging hardware.

MOLDING COMPOUND FRAME

MATERIALS:

- ½" (12 MM) MDF • HARD MOLDING COMPOUND
- STAR TIP AND DISPOSABLE CAKE DECORATING BAGS • PRIMER
- SPRAY PAINT • ANTIQUING GLAZE • 5¼ × 7¼" (134 × 184 MM) GLASS
- ¼" (6 MM) HARDBOARD • GLAZING POINTS • HANGING HARDWARE

1 Cut an 8 × 10 (203 × 254 mm) rectangle of MDF, and mark a 4½ × 6½" (115 × 165 mm) rectangle centered within. Drill a hole at each corner, and use a jig saw to cut out this center rectangle. If necessary, use a hammer and chisel to clean up the edges of the cutout. On the back, use a ⅜" (10 mm) straight bit to rout a channel at the edges of the cutout. Apply a coat of primer to all sides and edges of the frame, and let it dry thoroughly. Across the front, use a straightedge to draw straight lines, ½" (12 mm) apart. Fill the decorating bag with molding compound, and add a star tip. Pipe stars along each marked line, as close to

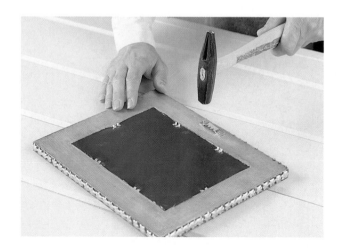

one another as possible. Let the compound dry for several hours. Working on one edge at a time, cover the edges of the frame with rows of stars. Let the compound dry for 48 hours.

2 Apply two coats of spray paint, letting the paint dry between coats. When the final coat is dry, brush antiquing glaze over the surface, then wipe away the excess with a clean cloth. Attach the hanging hardware on the back of the frame. Add glass, a photo or print, and a 5¼ × 7¼" piece of hardboard. Insert glazing points to hold the backing and glass in place.

EMBELLISHED FRAME

1 Select two inexpensive frames that complement one another. One must be larger than the other. (We bought these at a garage sale for 50 cents each.) Set one frame inside the other, and mark the corners of the smaller frame onto the larger one. Using a miter saw, cut the larger frame at the marked spots. It's best to err on the side of generosity, if at all. If the frame's slightly too large, you can trim it, but if it's too small, there's no way to make it work. Position the frame pieces, add wood glue to the joints, and secure them with a strap clamp. When the glue is dry, remove the clamp, and turn the frame over. Glue the smaller frame to the back of the larger one and let it dry. Fill any gaps with paintable latex caulk. Apply a coat of latex primer or pigmented shellac to the frame.

2 Assemble a disposable cake decorating bag with a coupler and leaf tip. Fill the bag with molding compound, and knead the compound to eliminate air pockets so it will flow smoothly. Pipe two leaves at each corner of the frame; switch to a beading tip and pipe a row of beading in a recess. (You may want to practice on paper first.) Let the compound dry thoroughly. Spray a coat of silver paint onto the frame and let it dry. If necessary, add a second coat. Apply a coat of antiquing glaze and let it set for a few minutes. Using a clean, dry cloth, remove the excess glaze. Leave enough glaze to enhance the frame's details. When the finish is dry, replace the original glass, backing, and hardware from the smaller frame.

MATERIALS:
• INEXPENSIVE FRAMES (2) • WOOD GLUE • PAINTABLE LATEX CAULK
• LEAF & BEADING TIPS • DISPOSABLE CAKE DECORATING BAGS
• HARD MOLDING COMPOUND • PRIMER • SPRAY PAINT
• ANTIQUING GLAZE

Accents

Accent pieces are the dessert of the decorating world. In the terms of my favorite Cajun cookbooks, they're *lagniappe*, the something extra that makes all that came before feel even more special. Even though they're not necessary in terms of a room's function, accents are essential ingredients because they provide precisely the little flourishes that are the hallmarks of cottage style.

Display your collections. Layer on colorful accents. Choose accessories that reflect your personality and interests. Find or make one-of-a-kind pieces that mark your home as uniquely your own. Remember, though, that too much of a good thing is just too much.

One good way to avoid overcrowding is to rotate accents with the seasons. Spring and fall are traditional times for deep cleaning. Why not add a change of accessories to that routine? Clean the old season's accents, then pack and store them. Arrange the pieces just coming out of storage and suddenly the room feels fresh and new. I find that bringing a favorite group of accents out of storage is like getting reacquainted with old friends.

   The seaside cottage above tells us that it's owned by people who love toys of all sizes, especially boats. The model boats and vintage toys displayed here are colorful counterpoints to the sitting room's spare white walls and furniture. Using a few large accents rather than dozens of smaller ones gives us a glimpse into the owners' lives without overwhelming the room.

   White wicker furniture set against a white beadboard ceiling and walls makes a perfect backdrop for the subtle colors of the accessories in the entryway at right. In addition to fresh and dried flowers, the room's accessories include bunnies, watering cans, and vintage children's books. Somehow you just know that door leads to a fabulous garden.

   Both rooms give us a sense of the lives lived within the cottages. To do this in your own home, choose accents that tell stories about who you are and what you care about.

Use accents to emphasize a room's color scheme or to blend a unique piece into its setting. In the bedroom at left, the colors in the upholstery fabrics, window treatments, and bed linens are replayed in the memory board, rug, and wall shelf—even the blue hippopotamus in the armchair takes part in this game.

The weathered pink paint of the cabinet in the dining room above might seem unusual, but surrounded by cranberry transferware plates and platters and some pink trim on the chair covers, it becomes an asset. If you find a unique piece that you really love, don't hesitate just because it might not go with your other furnishings. Instead, bring it home and then concentrate on selecting accents that will help it fit in.

Clocks

Cover a mantle or shelf with graceful clocks.

SPINDLE CLOCKS

MATERIALS:

- DECK OR STAIR BALUSTER OR NEWEL POST • WOOD GLUE
- DOWEL PINS • SPACKLE • CLOCK MOVEMENT OR SALVAGED WATCH FACE • LATEX PAINT OR MATERIALS FOR SPECIALTY FINISHES
- RUBBER O-RING • BRASS COAT HOOKS (OPTIONAL)

1 Study the baluster or post you've chosen and decide where to cut it and which portions to use to produce a well balanced shape. Mark cutting lines and cut the spindle apart. On each section to be joined, mark a centerpoint and drill a hole for a dowel pin. Spread wood glue on the mating surfaces, and use dowel pins to connect the sections. Fill any gaps with spackle, then sand the finished spindle.

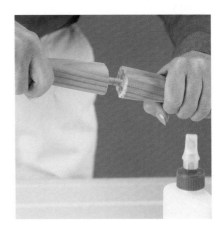

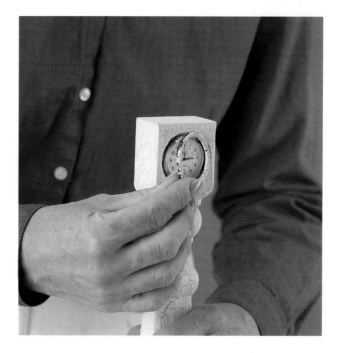

2 *Measure the watch face, and decide where to position it. Mark a centerpoint, then use a spade bit to drill an appropriate hole. Cut a base scaled to suit the baluster or post, drill a hole in the center of each, and join them with glue and dowel pins. Optional: Mark three equidistant points around the base, then attach one brass coat hook at each mark.*

3 *Paint the spindle or give it a decorative finish, such as metallic leaf. (For the baluster clocks, we used an undercoat of taupe, crackle medium and then ivory paint for a top coat. For the newel post clock, we used a yellow base coat topped with a pearl yellow glaze.) If you're using a watch face as shown here, paint an O-ring and use it as a retaining ring to hold the watch face in place.*

MANTLE CLOCK

MATERIALS:

• 2" (50 MM) RIGID FOAM INSULATION • VENEER PLYWOOD • CONSTRUCTION ADHESIVE • ½" (12 MM) MDF • DECORATIVE CORNER CAPS • WOOD APPLIQUE • ⅛" (4 MM) WOOD DOWEL • WOOD GLUE • WOODEN CANDLE CUPS • WOOD FILLER • PRIMER • LATEX PAINT OR SPECIALTY FINISH • 1-GALLON (3.8 L) PAINT CAN • 3" (75 MM) CLOCK MOVEMENT

1 *Cut 2 blocks of rigid foam, one 5¾ × 2" (145 × 50 mm), and one 5¼ × 5¾" (135 × 145 mm). Trace the arc from a 1 gallon paint can onto the 5¾ × 2" block and use a coping saw to cut out the bonnet.*

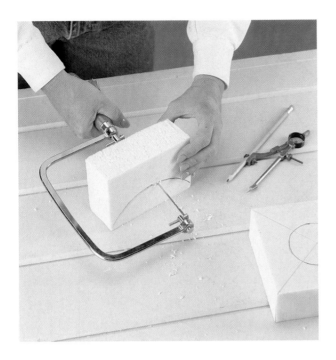

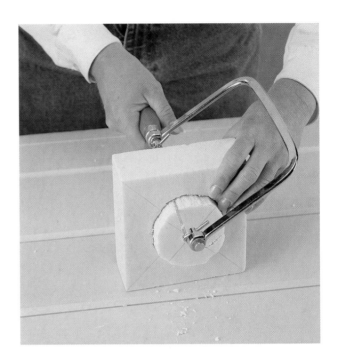

2 Use a protracter to scribe a 3" (75 mm) circle at the center of the block. Disassemble the coping saw, insert the blade through the foam, then reassemble the saw and cut along the marked line to cut the opening for the clock movement.

3 Trace the clock front and back of the body and the bonnet onto veneer plywood, and use a razor knife to cut out the pieces. Cut a 3" hole at the center of the front piece. Apply the veneer pieces to the blocks, using construction adhesive, such as Liquid Nails. For the arch of the bonnet, use masking tape to guide the veneer and to hold the veneer in place until the adhesive dries.

4 Cut four pieces of decorative corner cap, each piece 5¼" (135 mm) long. Glue one of these corner caps to each corner of the clock body; until the glue dries, hold the pieces in place with several rubber bands.

5 Cut two 7¾ × 4⅛" (200 × 105 mm) pieces of ½" MDF and rout the edges of each with a Roman ogee bit. On the bottom of one of the pieces of MDF (the base), drill a ⅛" (4 mm) pilot hole at each corner. Center the clock body between the cap and base, and use construction adhesive

to secure them. Let the adhesive dry thoroughly, then center the bonnet on the MDF cap and glue it in place. Cut four pieces of ⅛" dowel, each piece ¾" (20 mm) long. Glue these dowels into the pilot holes, and then glue the candlecup feet in place over them. Finally, center a candle cup at the top of the bonnet and glue it in place.

6 Glue a wood applique to the center of the bonnet. Apply wood filler to all gaps and let it dry. Lightly sand the clock, apply a coat of primer, and let it dry. Finish as desired. (We painted ours with Powder Blue Americana Satin paint by DecoArt.) Insert the clock movement.

BONNET

CAP

BASE

FEET

DECORATION CORNER CAPS

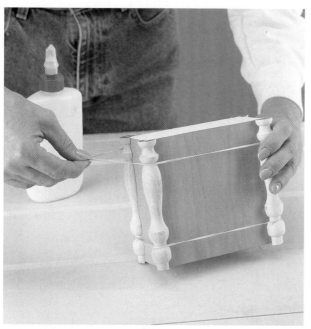

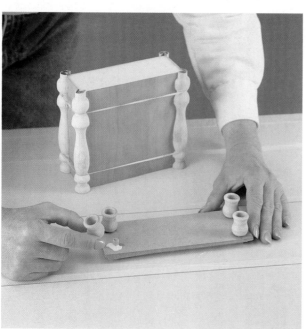

HALF MOON MANTLE CLOCK

1 Cut a 6¾ × 3⅜" (170 × 85 mm) block of rigid foam. Center the arc of a 1-gallon paint can on the block, and lightly scribe its shape into the foam.

2 Center the clock movement on the foam body and trace its shape. Cut out the marked circle (see step 2 on page 93). Trace the front and back of the foam block onto plywood veneer; draw a 2¹⁄₁₆ × 10¼" (52 × 260 mm) rectangle as well. Cut out the veneer; cut out a 3" (76 mm) hole centered in the front piece. Glue the veneer to the front, back, and top with construction adhesive. Hold the top in place with masking tape until the adhesive is dry. Cut a 8⅜ × 3½" (215 × 90 mm) piece of MDF for the base and rout the edges with a Roman ogee bit. Remove the tape, center the body on the base, and glue it in place. Fill any gaps at the edges and corners with wood filler. Add the feet, knob, and face decorations (see step 5 on page 93). Lightly sand the entire assembly, then apply a coat of primer. When the primer is dry, paint the clock and let it dry. (We used Light Willow Americana Satin paint by DecoArt then sponged on a yellow glaze.) Install the clock movement.

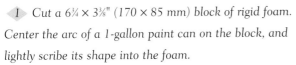

FLOOR CLOTH

Drab floors? Paint a simple floor cloth to add a charming spot of color.

◈ *1* *Cut a 30 × 34" (76 cm × 91 cm) piece of sheet vinyl. Enlarge the pattern on page 133 and transfer it to the sheet vinyl (see page 125). Use heavy-duty scissors to cut along the marked lines.*

◈ *2* *Roll a coat of latex-based primer onto the back side of the sheet vinyl. When the primer is dry, apply two coats of white latex paint. When the paint is dry, mask off a checkerboard pattern; paint the inside edges of the tape with matte medium and let it dry. (This keeps the paint from seeping under the tape as you paint.)*

◈ *3* *Paint alternating squares with Touch O' Pink, let the paint dry, and remove the tape. Paint the Eucalyptus and then the Mulberry border. When the paint is dry, use a white paint pen to add a narrow border between the green and the mulberry. Stencil or stamp a raspberry in every other white square, using Eucalyptus for the stems and Mulberry for the berries. Let the paint dry for a week, then apply two coats of polyurethane.*

MATERIALS:

• Scrap of sheet vinyl flooring • Latex-based primer
• Masking tape • Matte medium • Delta Ceramacoat paint,
Touch O' Pink, Eucalyptus Green, and Mulberry
• White latex paint • White paint pen
• Raspberry stencil • Water-based polyurethane

MINIATURE WIRE TABLE & CHAIR

Twist copper wire into a table and chair that hold plants and candles.

1 For the legs, mark the midpoint of each 16" wire. Clamp a 10 to 12" (255 to 305 mm) scrap of ½" (12 mm) copper pipe into a workbench. Working with one piece of wire at a time, center the marked point over the top of the ½" pipe. Bend the wire around the pipe and twist it tightly; make 2 to 2½ additional twists, then remove the wire from the form. Use a pair of pliers to straighten the tails and make sure they are parallel to one another. Two inches from the ends, bend the tails in opposite directions. Also, bend the loop forward to form a foot. Set the legs aside.

2 For the chair back, mark the midpoint of the 24" wire, then wrap it all the way around a 1-gallon paint can. Crimp the wire at the marked point, then pull the ends in opposite directions until a 1½" (40 mm) loop is formed at the center.

Part	Material	Length	No.
Chair legs	8-gauge copper wire	16" (400 mm)	4
Chair back	8-gauge copper wire	24" (600 mm)	1
Chair seat	⅜" copper tubing	20" (500 mm)	1
Table legs	8-gauge copper wire	24" (600 mm)	3
Tabletop	⅜" copper tubing	30" (750 mm)	1
Table leg supports	¼" copper tubing	15" (375 mm)	2

MATERIALS:
- 8-GAUGE (4 MM) COPPER WIRE • ⅜" (10 MM) FLEXIBLE COPPER TUBING
- ¼" (8 MM) FLEXIBLE COPPER TUBING • SCRAP OF ½" (12 MM) RIGID COPPER PIPE • 5" (130 MM) POT AND SAUCER • 2½" PVC PIPE
- 1-GALLON (3.8 L) PAINT CAN • EMPTY QUART PAINT CANS (2)
- 20-GAUGE (0.8 MM) COPPER WIRE • FLUX • SOLDER

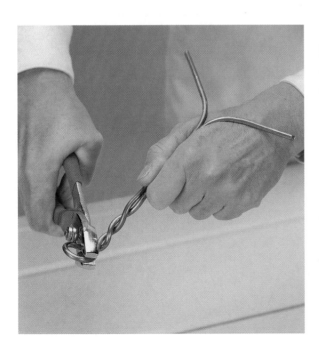

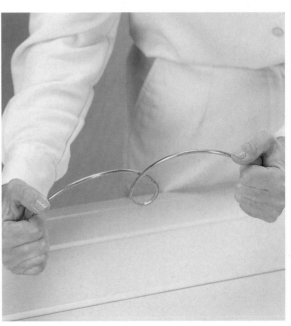

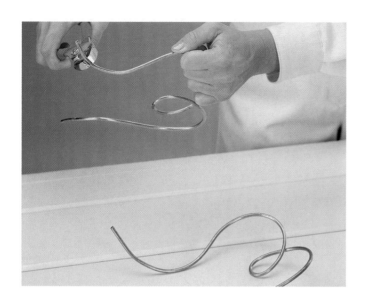

3 Form the ends of the looped wire into arches running in the opposite directions. Set the back aside.

4 For the seat, wrap the 20" piece of ⅜" tubing around the 5" saucer, just under the saucer's rim. (The tubing should extend around the saucer about 1¼ times.) At the overlap, cut through both pieces of tubing, using a jig saw. Open the circle slightly, and flare one end of the tubing with a flaring tool.

5 Clean the ends of the tubing and of the wire pieces. Place a 12" (305 mm) ceramic tile or other heatproof surface at the edge of the table. Flux the flared joint of the seat, and the tails of each leg. Place the legs over the seat and prop them in place. Flux the tails of the chair back

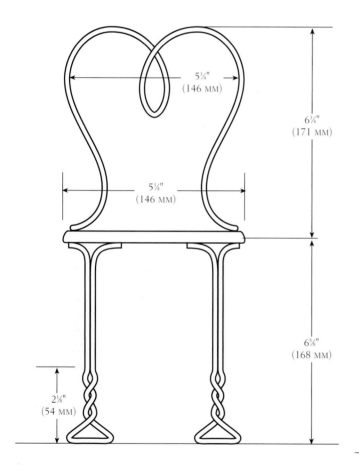

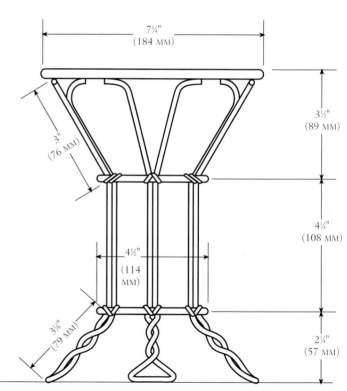

and position it so the back hangs upside down, over the edge of the tile. Place the seat over the tails to hold them in place. Solder the joints, then clean up all the pieces with steel wool.

6 To make the three table legs, mark the midpoint of the 24" wires and shape them as directed in Step 1. Bend the loops to form feet as in step 1. About 3½" (90 mm) from the end, bend each leg up to form a foot.

For the tabletop, wrap the 30" piece of ⅜" tubing around the rim of the 5" pot. Complete the process as described in Step 4. Follow the same procedure to create two support rings from the 15" pieces of ¼" tubing, shaping the rings around a scrap piece of 2½" PVC pipe. Assemble the pieces of the table as described in Step 5, except: Wrap 20-gauge wire around the support rings and legs to hold them in place. Clean, flux, and solder the joints.

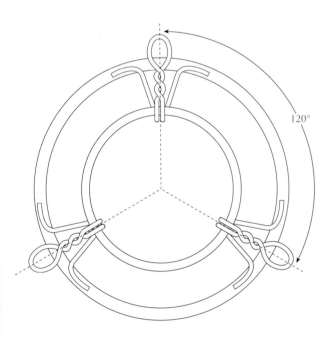

120°

TABLE: PLAN VIEW FROM BOTTOM

DISPLAY SHELF

Dress a simple shelf in Victorian-style gingerbread.

1 *Cut the parts as indicated below. Miter the corners of the side and front trim. Spread wood glue over the surface of one of the shelf supports, clamp the second shelf support to it, and let the glue dry. Attach the shelf back to the shelf supports with screws driven about every 6" (155 mm). (See diagram on page 135.)*

2 *Spread glue along the top of the shelf back and the top of the shelf support. Position this assembly over the shelf and attach it with screws driven every 6".*

3 *Run a bead of Liquid Nails along the first 1½" (40 cm) and corners of the front and side trim, and clamp it in place. Drive a screw through the shelf and into the trim about every 6" along the front and sides. When the adhesive is dry, prime and paint the shelf as desired. Add sturdy hanging hardware.*

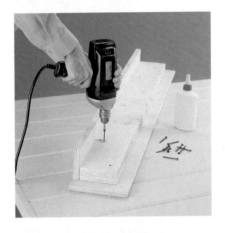

Part	Size	Number
Solid core veneer plywood:		
Shelf	6½ × 43" (165 × 1090 mm)	1
Shelf supports	4¼ × 40" (110 × 1020 mm)	2
Shelf back	3½ × 40" (90 × 1020 mm)	1
Decorative trim:		
Side trim	6" (155 mm)	2
Front trim	42" (1070 mm)	1

Note: these dimensions are for decorative trim with a 6" repeat, such as this scalloped molding (part # MLD640-8) from Architectural Products by Outwater Industries. (See page 141 for details.)

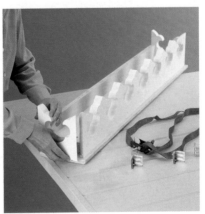

MATERIALS:

- ½" (12 mm) SOLID CORE VENEER PLYWOOD
- DECORATIVE TRIM (8 FT. [2400 mm]) • WOOD GLUE
- 1½" (35 mm) WOOD SCREWS • LIQUID NAILS
- LATEX PAINT

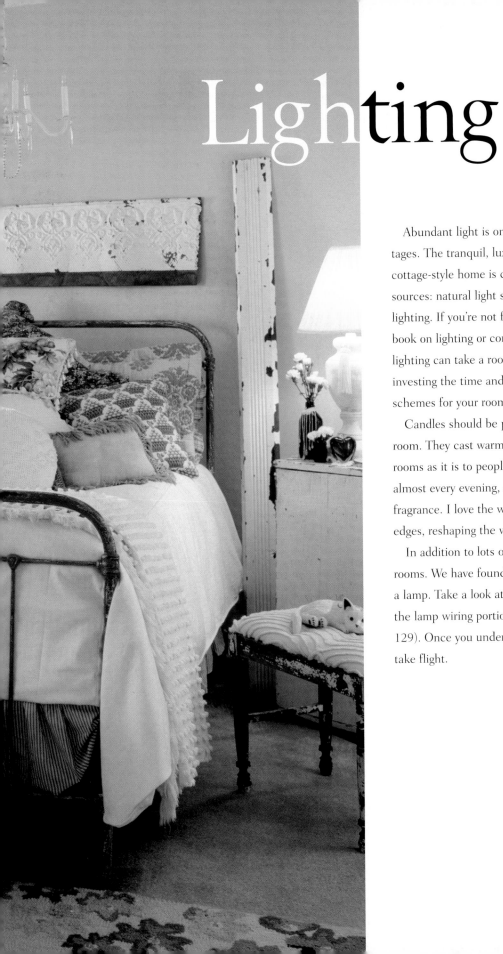

Lighting

Abundant light is one of the main characteristics of cottages. The tranquil, luxurious type of lighting that defines a cottage-style home is created by a combination of light sources: natural light supplemented by fill, accent and task lighting. If you're not familiar with these terms, find a good book on lighting or consult a lighting specialist. The right lighting can take a room from nice to splendid, so it's worth investing the time and money to develop effective lighting schemes for your rooms.

Candles should be part of the plan for every cottage-style room. They cast warm, gentle light that's as flattering to rooms as it is to people. Tim, whose family lights candles almost every evening, says that he particularly enjoys their fragrance. I love the way their flickering light softens the edges, reshaping the world within their glow.

In addition to lots of candles, add special lamps to your rooms. We have found that almost anything can be made into a lamp. Take a look at the lamp projects in this section and the lamp wiring portion of the Techniques section (page 129). Once you understand the basics, let your imagination take flight.

During the day, sunshine streaming through the windows fills the bedroom above, as well as the sitting room at right, with light. At night, the glass provides a reflective surface for the lamp light. In the bedroom, window treatments were selected to soften the windows without interfering with the light they provide. In the sitting room, the windows are dressed only by the foliage right outside their panes.

The sitting room's track lighting focuses attention on the framed print and the plate collection displayed behind the sofa, emphasizing their colors and details. Track lighting is a good, affordable option for spotlighting special pieces. Individual heads can be aimed directly at favorite objects, bathing them in pools of light that mark them as special and significant.

If a room includes valuable art or vintage fabrics, be especially careful about the type and placement of the lighting—some types of lighting can cause fading or discoloration. Many lighting stores have specialists who can give you advice and guidance on the subject.

Back in the days when candles were extremely expensive, mirrors and glass were used to reflect and multiply their precious light. It still works today. In the patio at left, light is reflected by dozens of glass votives, hurricane globes, and other candleholders. The glassware reflects the glow of the flames and lends a special air of mystery, magic, and romance to this outdoor room.

The fitting or shade you select has a significant impact on the quality of light produced by any lamp or light fixture. The opaque glass of the table lamp above (left) diffuses the light to produce a warm glow. In the bedroom above (right), the lamplight is filtered by a piece of silk organza layered over the white cloth shade. When you're selecting shades, keep in mind the style and shape of the lamp, the tone of the room, and the effect you want to create with each particular lamp.

Having the right type of light in the right places makes a room more comfortable and efficient as well as more attractive. For most circumstances, the following guidelines will produce well-lit rooms.

• The lower edge of the shade on a table lamp should be at eye level when you're seated—about 38 to 42" (950 to 1050 mm) above the floor.

• The lower edge of the shade on floor lamps should be about 40 to 48" (1000 to 1230 mm) from the floor.

• Taller lamps used for reading should be positioned 15" (380 mm) to the side and 20" (510 mm) behind the center of the book when you're reading.

• Chandeliers should be suspended 34 to 36" (850 to 900 mm) above the surface of the table in dining areas, and well above a person's height in hallways and other walking areas.

TEAPOT LAMP

Brighten an occasional table or writing desk with a lamp made from a tea-for-one.

1 *Center and drill a ½" (12 mm) hole in the cup and pot of a tea-for-one. (The one we used is by Tracy Porter.) Support each piece in a container of sand; use a rotary tool and a silicon carbide grinding stone. If the lid has a handle, use the rotary tool and a cut-off disc to cut a ⅝" (15 mm) opening in it. Finally, drill a ½" hole through the center of the lid.*

2 *Slide a lock washer and a hex nut onto one end of a threaded brass rod. Insert the rod into the hole of the lamp base and add a lock washer and hex nut below the base. Tighten the nuts against one another until the rod is stable. Put the rod through the hole in the cup and position the cup on the base. Squirt a bead of silicone caulk around the edges of the hole to make a buffer between the rod and the china. Add the teapot and put silicone around its hole. Thread a coupler and a second brass rod onto the first, then add the teapot's lid. Add silicone around the hole in the lid.*

3 *Top the brass rod with a threaded brass washer, a harp, another threaded brass washer, and a socket cap. Insert a lamp cord through the base and up through the top. Tie the split ends of the wire in an underwriter's knot, connect them to the lamp socket, and assemble the socket (see page 129). Add a lampshade, and if desired, a finial.*

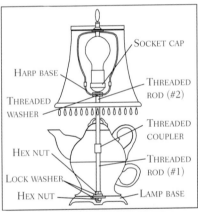

SOCKET CAP

HARP BASE

THREADED ROD (#2)

THREADED WASHER

THREADED COUPLER

HEX NUT

THREADED ROD (#1)

LOCK WASHER

HEX NUT

LAMP BASE

MATERIALS:

• TEA-FOR-ONE • BRASS LAMP BASE • LOCK WASHERS (2)
• HEX NUTS (2) • 5" (130 MM) THREADED BRASS LAMP ROD (2)
• SILICONE CAULK • 1" (25 MM) BRASS COUPLER • THREADED BRASS
WASHERS (2) • HARP • SOCKET CAP • LAMP SOCKET
• LAMP CORD • LAMPSHADE

TEACUP CANDLE

Add a bit of sparkle with this delightful project.

1 *Slowly melt the wax, using a double boiler. Prime a length of wick by dipping it into melted wax for a few seconds and then allowing it to cool. Stick the end of a primed wick into a wick sustainer, and use needlenose pliers to crimp the metal around the wick. Tie the wick to a stir stick, then set the stick across the teacup. Carefully pour melted wax into the teacup, filling it about two-thirds full. When the wax has solidified, trim the wick to extend approximately ⅝" (16 mm) above the candle's surface.*

2 *Glue the teacup to the saucer, using two-part epoxy. Mark three equidistant points around the bottom of the saucer; glue a shelf hanger to the saucer at each marked point. Cut three 15" (380 mm) lengths of chain. Using needlenose pliers to open the appropriate links, divide each 15" chain into three equal sections. Using several beads strung onto an eye pin or a short string of prisms, reconnect the chain and close the links. End each chain with a beaded eye pin or a string of prisms. At the non-beaded end of each chain, open the last link, thread it through the shelf hanger, and close the link securely.*

3 *Glue a beaded tassel or crystal pendant at the center of the bottom of the saucer. Cut a 9" (230 mm) length of chain; use an eye pin to link the beaded chains to one another and then to the 9" chain. Suspend the teacup candle from a sturdy hook.*

MATERIALS:

• TEACUP AND SAUCER • CANDLE WICK • WICK SUSTAINER • PARAFFIN WAX • TWO-PART EPOXY • BRASS DOUBLE-JACK CHAIN (5 FEET [1525 M]) • BEADS OR CRYSTAL PRISMS • EYE PINS • BRASS SHELF HANGERS OR FRAME HANGER D-STRAPS (3) • BEADED TASSLE OR CRYSTAL PENDANT

REFURBISHED CHANDELIER

Not just for dining areas anymore! Let chandeliers sparkle in unexpected places.

1 *Remove the light bulbs and sleeves from the sockets of the chandelier. Drill a hole at the front, back and each side of each candle cup. Mark equally spaced holes around the perimeter of the rosette, each hole corresponding to an arm of the chandelier. If necessary, use a flat file or a rotary tool to polish away any rough edges on the holes.*

2 *Tape off the sockets, and rough up the chandelier's surface with coarse steel wool. Spray paint the entire chan-* *delier with two coats of base coat and let it dry. Holding the can within 8" (200 mm) of the surface, spray a moderately heavy layer of top coat onto the entire chandelier. (We used Plasti-kote's Cracklin' Gold base coat and Cream top coat. Read and follow manufacturer's directions for the product you select.) When the paint is dry, remove the masking tape from the sockets.*

MATERIALS:
• SALVAGED CHANDELIER • MASKING TAPE
• CRACKLE FINISH SPRAY PAINT BASE COAT AND TOP COAT
• CRYSTAL PENDANTS • STRANDS OF PRISM BEADS
• DECORATIVE LAMPSHADES

3 *Attach a strand of prism beads to a hole in the rosette and to the back of the corresponding candle cup. Experiment to find a length that allows the strand to droop gracefully. Cut additional strands of the same length, and attach one to each remaining set of holes.*

4 *Attach a strand of beads to the side of one candle cup and loop it toward the adjoining candle cup. Again, experiment to find a graceful length. Cut additional strands of the same length, and attach them between the arms.*

5 *Hang a crystal pendant from the hole in the front of each candle cup. Replace the sleeves and light bulbs, and add lampshades.*

Note: You can purchase inexpensive chandeliers from home centers, garage sales, and flea markets. We rescued this one from the center of a Tiffany-style fixture that had been discarded. We found the prisms and much more online at Chandelierparts.com.

Making Decorative Lampshades

You can find a wide variety of decorative lampshades for chandeliers these days,
but it may be less expensive to create your own.

For each, you'll need a self adhesive lampshade, fabric, and decorative trim. Check the label on the lampshades for yardage requirements.

The paper protector on a self-adhesive shade also acts as a pattern. Peel the protector from the shade, and trace it onto your fabric, adding 1" (25 mm) all around for the seam allowance.

Next, cut out the fabric and place the wrong side on the shade, with the seam allowances extending past the top, bottom, and seam. Press the fabric onto the shade, and smooth it from side to side and top to bottom to eliminate ripples or wrinkles. Trim the seams to ⅜" (10 mm), and use white glue to secure the overlapping seam.

Clip the top edge of the fabric every ½" (12 mm), then roll the seam allowance snugly over the wire edge and hot glue it to the inside of the shade. Roll the seam allowance snugly over the bottom edge and glue it to the inside of the shade as well.

Starting and stopping at the seam and gluing about 2" (50 mm) at a time, glue decorative trim to the edge of the shade.

GILDED CANDLESTICKS

A perfect example of trash to treasure: discarded balusters or bed posts become candlesticks.

1 Cut the baluster or bed post into two equal segments. In deciding where to cut, consider scale and proportion, and remember that the bottom of the finished candlestick needs to be heavier than the top. Drill a 1" (25 mm) hole in the center of the top of each candlestick, then lightly sand the surfaces.

2 Apply a base coat to each candlestick and let it dry. (We used Delta's Renaissance Foil Easy Crackle System.) Coat each candlestick with a coat of adhesive, and let it dry. Add a second coat of adhesive in an opposite or cross-wise direction. Let the adhesive dry for about an hour, or until it's clear and tacky. Lay a small piece of foil leaf onto an area, shiny side up, and burnish it with your finger or a smooth rubber tool. Push the foil firmly into hard-to-reach areas. Peel the foil away from its base and continue adding pieces of leaf, overlapping as necessary. To avoid creases and wrinkles, it's best to use small pieces on the curves and turned areas. Let the candlesticks dry for at least one hour.

3 Apply a heavy coat of crackle medium, using a soft bristle brush. Let the crackle medium dry for 24 hours; cracks will develop in the first hour or so. Spray a coat of sealer on each candlestick and let it dry. Apply a coat of antiquing glaze, and remove as much as desired, using a clean, soft cloth.

MATERIALS:

• SALVAGED BALUSTER OR BEDPOST • BASE COAT • ADHESIVE
• GOLD OR SILVER FOIL • CRACKLE MEDIUM • SEALER
• ANTIQUING GLAZE

BALUSTER LAMP

Join balusters to form a column that becomes a lovely floor lamp.

1 *If the balusters are finished, sand or strip them. (If you're dealing with paint from before 1978, follow precautions for lead paint.) Measure the balusters and determine which portions to use (see page 134). Mark and cut the balusters into four sections, each approximately 10" (250 mm) long.*

2 *Use an auger bit to drill a ½" (12 mm) hole through the center of each baluster section. Stack the first two sections, then mark and drill a ½"-deep ¼" (6 mm) hole on each face of the joint, one to each side of the center hole. Glue dowel pins into these holes, spread glue on the faces of the joint, and clamp the sections together. When the glue is dry, proceed to the next joint. When the pieces are assembled, fill any gaps with wood filler and sand as necessary.*

3 *For the base, cut a 12" (305 mm) square of MDF, and rout the edges with a Roman ogee bit. Drill a ½" hole through the center of the base, then countersink it by drilling a 1"-diameter (25 mm) hole ⅜" (9 mm) deep and centered around the original hole. For the feet, drill pilot holes and screw a candlecup ½" in from each corner. Finish the baluster and base as desired. (We used primer and two coats of latex paint.) Join the 36" threaded rod to the 12" rod with a brass coupler. Thread a lock washer and a hex nut about ¾" (19 mm) up the end of the rod, and insert it down through the base. Put a flat brass washer, a lock washer, and a hex nut on the bottom of the threaded rod and tighten the nuts against one another. Put the baluster over the rod and center it on top of the base.*

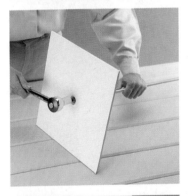

4 *Top the rod with a threaded brass washer, then thread the brass collars onto it. Add a threaded brass washer and then a harp; attach a socket cap. Pull the lamp cord through the rod and into the socket cap. Tie the split ends of the wire in an underwriter's knot, connect them to the lamp socket, and assemble the socket (see page 129). Add a lamp shade, and if you like, a finial.*

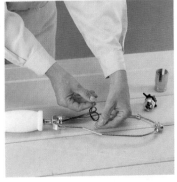

MATERIALS:

- SALVAGED BALUSTERS (2) • ¼" (6 MM) DOWEL PINS • WOOD GLUE
- LATEX WOOD FILLER • ¾" (19 MM) MDF • 1" (25 MM) WOODEN CANDLECUPS (4)
- ½" (12 MM) SCREWS • PAINT OR STAIN • THREADED RODS (ONE 36" [914 MM], ONE 12" [305 MM]) • 1 BRASS COUPLER • FLAT BRASS WASHER • LOCK WASHERS (2)
- HEX NUTS (2) • THREADED BRASS WASHERS (2) • 1" (25 MM) BRASS COLLARS (2)
- HARP • SOCKET CAP • LAMP SOCKET • LAMP CORD • LAMPSHADE

Techniques

A few tips and tricks to help you get started.

KNIFE-EDGE PILLOWS

Cut two pieces of fabric 1" (25 mm) larger in both directions than the desired finished size of the pillow. For example, cut two 17" (430mm) squares for a 16" (405 mm) pillow; cut two 13 × 19" (330 × 485 mm) rectangles for a 12 × 18" (305 × 460 mm) pillow.

Place the front over the back, right sides together, and align all four edges. Pin the layers together. In the

center of one side, leave a 7" (180 mm) opening unpinned.

Using a ½" (12 mm) seam allowance and starting just ahead of the opening, backstitch three or four stitches, then stitch around all four sides, pivoting with the needle down at the corners. End the seam at the opposite side of the opening; backstitch three or four stitches. Trim the threads close to the fabric, then press the seams flat to set the stitching line.

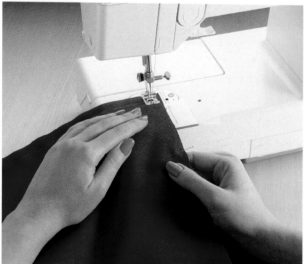

Turn back the top seam allowance, and press, applying light pressure with the tip of the iron down the crease of the seam. In the area of the opening, turn back and press ½" to match the top seam allowance. Turn the fabric over; turn back and press the remaining opening seam allowance.

At a corner, fold two seam allowances in, and then fold the other two seam allowances over them. Slip four fingers through the pillow opening and pinch the folded corner between your thumb and one finger. Turn that corner through the opening. Repeat with the other three corners to turn the pillow cover right side out.

Compress and insert the pillow form. Align the pressed edges of the opening, and pin the opening closed. Using a hand needle and thread, slip stitch the opening closed.

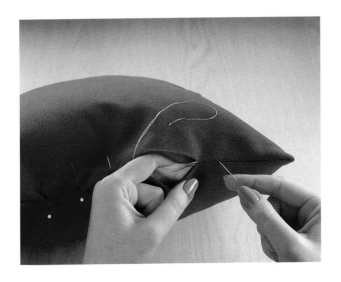

PILLOW FRINGE

Mark a line around the pillow front, ½" (12 mm) from the edge. Align the edge of the fringe with the mark and pin it to the pillow top, easing it around the corners. Fold back ¾" (19 mm) at each end; butt the folded ends. Machine-baste the fringe in place. Add the pillow back, and pin; leave a 7" (180 mm) opening. Starting and ending at the opening, sew the layers together. Trim the seam allowances diagonally across corners; do not cut through the fringe. Press the seams open, then turn the pillow cover right side out. Gently pull the fringe to shape the corners. Insert the form, pin and slip stitch the opening.

ENLARGING & TRANSFERRING PATTERNS

The first step in many projects is enlarging and transferring a pattern. Copy centers often have large-capacity machines and knowledgeable staff. Their help can be expensive, though, so check prices before you start.

If you have access to a photocopier and need a pattern within its range, follow the instructions on the copier. If you need larger patterns, enlarge your enlargements until you reach the size you need. If you need a pattern larger than the largest paper used by a standard copier (typically 11 × 17"), use a process known as tiling. First, make registration marks on the original, then enlarge and copy one section at a time. Lay out the copies, match the registration marks, and tape the pieces into a full-size pattern.

An overhead projector is a valuable tool for enlarging and transferring patterns. Start by photocopying the pattern onto a transparency. (One product we've used successfully is Transparency Film for Copiers by 3M.) Put the media into the paper supply of a copier and make a copy as usual. Tape butcher paper—or the project itself—onto a wall, and project the image onto it. Move the projector closer to or further from the wall until the image reaches the correct size, then trace the projected image.

Graphite Paper: Buy a high quality, smudgeproof product and treat it gently. Put the graphite paper under the pattern and trace with a dull pencil or stylus. We like graphite paper but have found the term "smudgeproof" somewhat optimistic. No matter what brand you use, handle it carefully and avoid touching it with anything other than the tip of the pencil as you trace.

Black and White Photocopies: The heat from an ordinary household iron on a cotton setting is enough to transfer toner from the photocopy onto the project's surface. This works on fabric and wood, especially. A few things to keep in mind: • Tape the pattern down so it will remain in place as you press. • Use a dry iron—steam could damage the project's surface. • Work quickly enough to avoid scorching the paper or the project. • Press in one spot, then lift the iron and move it to the next spot. (Sliding the iron increases the chances of moving or blurring the pattern.) • Let painted surfaces dry for at least 48 hours first.

Pounce Bag: Poke a series of small holes along the lines of a paper pattern. Fill the bag with chalk and pounce it along those lines. The chalk will filter through the holes and create a pattern on the surface. This method is suitable for large-scale projects with simple lines.

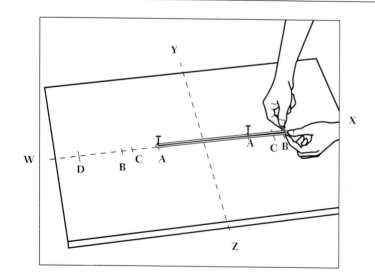

MAKING OVALS

To make an oval cutout frame with outside dimensions of 22½" × 27" (572 × 686 mm) and inside dimensions of 13¾" × 17¾" (350 × 450 mm):

Cut ½" MDF to 25" × 32" (635 × 814 mm). Divide the board into equal quadrants to find the center (lines WX and YZ).

From the center, measure out along line WX:

4¹⁵⁄₁₆" (125 mm) and mark points A

8⅞" (225 mm) and mark points B

7¾" (197 mm) and mark points C

13½" (342 mm) and mark points D.

Drive 1" (25 mm) brads at points A. Cut a 30" (762 mm) cord, wrap the cord around both brads and tie off at point B. Slip a pencil inside cord. Holding the pencil vertically, scribe one half of the ellipse. Move the pencil and cord to the other side of the brads and scribe the second half of the ellipse.

Transfer brads from points A to points C. Cut a 48" (1220 mm) cord and tie off at point D. Repeat the scribing technique for both halves of the outer ellipse.

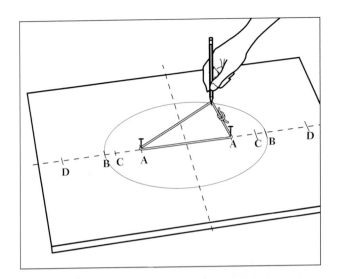

SOLDERING

Soldering, or sweating, joints is much easier than you might imagine. If propane torches intimidate you, try one of the new, compact versions. The smaller size and quieter burn may feel more comfortable while you're learning. To solder a joint, you use a propane torch to heat a copper or brass fitting until it's just hot enough to melt the solder. The heat then draws the solder into the gap between the fitting and the pipe, forming a strong seal.

As with many do-it-yourself tasks, you'll find that good preparation makes everything else much easier. To form a strong joint, the ends of the pipes and the insides of the fittings must be clean and smooth. Soldering copper isn't difficult, but it requires some patience and skill. It's a good idea to practice on scrap pipe before taking on a large project.

The most common mistake beginners make is using too much heat. To avoid this problem, remember that the tip of the torch's inner flame produces the most heat. Direct the flame carefully—solder will flow in the direction the heat has traveled. Heat the pipe just until the flux sizzles; remove the flame and touch the solder to the pipe. The heated pipe will quickly melt the solder.

Plan to work on a heat-resistant surface or on a double layer of 26-gauge (0.5 mm) sheet metal. The sheet metal makes an effective shield, and its reflective quality helps the joints heat evenly.

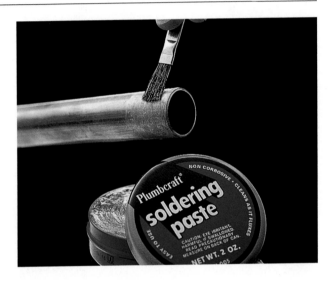

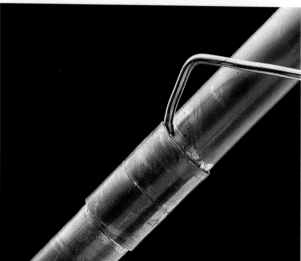

If a series of pipe and fittings (a run) is involved, dry-fit the entire run before soldering any of the joints. When the run is correctly assembled, take it apart and prepare to solder the joints.

Sand the ends of the pipes with emery cloth and scour the insides of the fittings with a wire brush. Apply a thin layer of water-soluble paste flux to the end of each pipe, using a flux brush. The flux should cover about 1" (25 mm) of the end of the pipe. Insert the pipe into the fitting until the pipe is tight against the fitting socket. Twist the fitting slightly to spread the flux.

When you're ready to solder, unwind 8 to 10" (200 to 250 mm) of solder from the spool. Bend the first 2" (50 mm) of the solder to a 90° angle.

Light the torch and adjust the valve until the inner portion of the flame is 1 to 2" (25 to 50 mm) long. Hold the flame tip against the middle of the fitting for 4 to 5 seconds or until the flux begins to sizzle. Heat the other side of the joint, distributing the heat evenly. Move the flame around the joint in the direction the solder should flow. Touch the solder to the pipe, just below the fitting. If it melts, the joint is hot enough.

Quickly apply solder along both seams of the fitting, allowing capillary action to draw the liquefied solder into the fitting. When the joint is filled, solder will begin to form droplets on the bottom of the joint. A correctly soldered joint shows a thin bead of silver-colored solder around the lip of the fitting. It typically takes about ½" (12 mm) of solder to fill a joint in ½" (12 mm) pipe.

Note: Always turn off the torch immediately after you've finished soldering; make sure the gas valve is completely closed.

Let the joint sit undisturbed until the solder loses its shiny color—don't touch it before then—the copper will be quite hot. When the joint is cool enough to touch, wipe away excess flux and solder, using a clean, dry rag. When the joint is cool, check for gaps around the edges. If it's not a good seal, take the joint apart and resolder it.

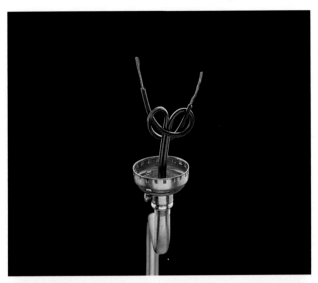

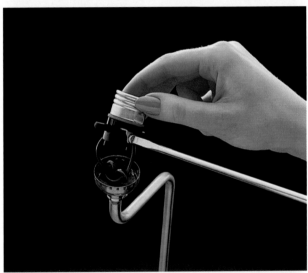

WIRING LAMPS

The first time I made a lamp, I was surprised by how easy it was to do the wiring. I guess it seemed mysterious and complicated because I had no idea how few steps it really takes. Basically, all you have to do is thread the lamp cord through the base and up to the socket, and then connect two wires. Very simple—it will probably take less than half an hour to do the whole thing, even the first time. The next time, it will take just a matter of minutes.

Thread the lamp cord through the base and up through the lamp pipe and socket cap. (Many lamp cords are pre-split and the ends are stripped in preparation for wiring. If yours isn't, use a utility knife to split the first 2" [50 mm] of the end of the cord, along the midline of the insulation. Strip about ½ to ¾" [12 to 19 mm] of insulation from the ends of the wires.)

Tie an underwriter's knot by forming an overhand loop with one wire and an underhand loop with the remaining wire; insert each wire end through the loop of the other wire.

Loosen the terminal screws on the socket. Look carefully at the insulation on the wires—the insulation on one wire will be rounded and on the other wire it will be ribbed or will have a fine line on it. Loop the wire on the rounded side around the socket's brass screw and tighten the screw. Loop the wire on the other side around the socket's silver screw and tighten the screw.

Adjust the underwriter's knot to fit within the base of the socket cap, then position the socket into the socket cap. Slide the insulating sleeve and outer shell over the socket so the terminal screws are fully covered and any slots are correctly aligned.

Test the lamp; when you're sure it works, press the socket assembly down into the socket cap until the socket locks into place.

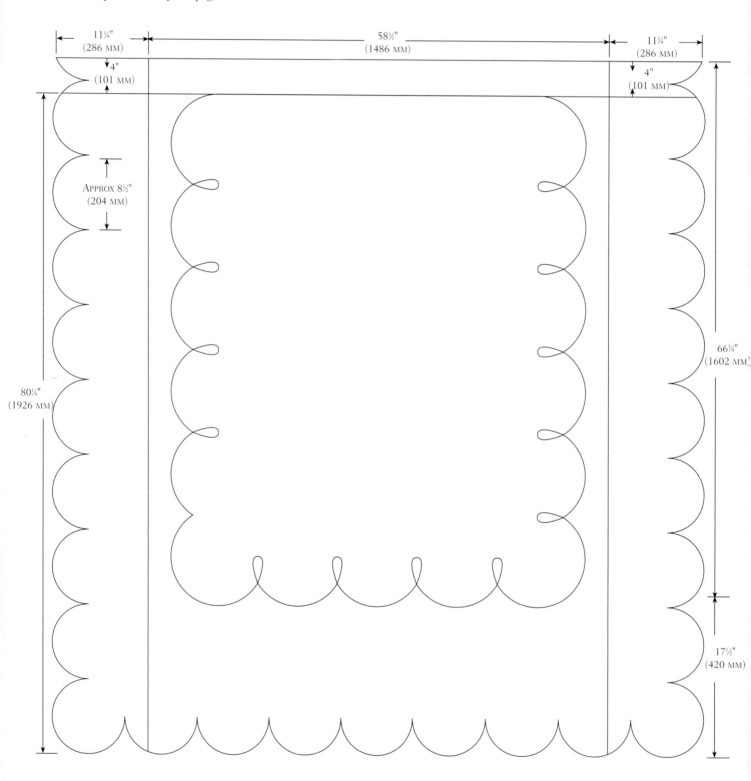

11¼"
(286 MM)

58½"
(1486 MM)

11¼"
(286 MM)

4"
(101 MM)

4"
(101 MM)

APPROX 8½"
(204 MM)

80¼"
(1926 MM)

66¾"
(1602 MM)

17½"
(420 MM)

60"
(1524 мм)

3" × 3" × 3" × 3"
(76 мм)

72"
(1829 мм)

Drop Leaf Table — enlarge by 300%
from page 34

Script Pillow Pattern — enlarge by 175%
from page 59

Baluster Floor lamp
from page 121

Baluster Cuts

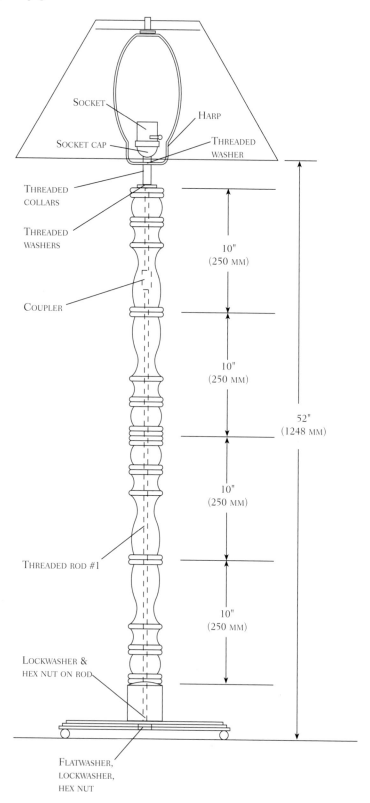

SOCKET

HARP

SOCKET CAP

THREADED WASHER

THREADED COLLARS

THREADED WASHERS

COUPLER

10"
(250 MM)

10"
(250 MM)

52"
(1248 MM)

10"
(250 MM)

THREADED ROD #1

10"
(250 MM)

LOCKWASHER & HEX NUT ON ROD

10"
(250 MM)

FLATWASHER,
LOCKWASHER,
HEX NUT

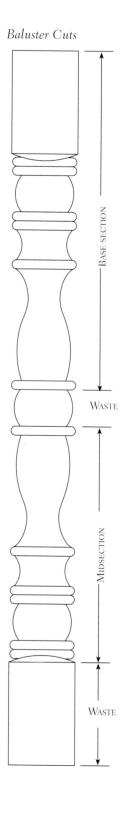

BASE SECTION

WASTE

MIDSECTION

WASTE

Glass-top Table Pattern — enlarge by 120%

Display Shelf

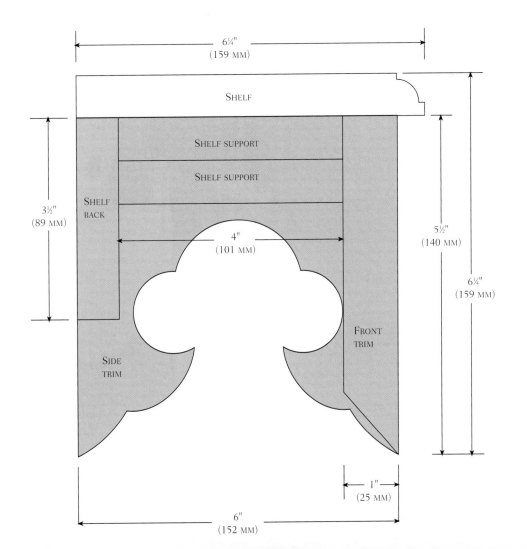

$\mathcal{A}$FTERWORD

It's the middle of the night, and I'm back in the Land of Oz, almost a year to the day since I first met Dorothy and Toto and discovered their enchanted world. *Cottage Style* is nearly done, and we're all very proud of it. My only problem is that I've found no conclusion, no graceful way to say good-bye.

Sitting in the new hot tub behind "Glinda's Cottage," surrounded by fairy lights twinkling through the vines that frame the autumn ghost of the garden, words from a poem by E.E. Cummings ran through my head. They are, I suddenly recognized, words that perfectly describe a cottage-style home:

"here is the deepest secret nobody knows
(here is the root of the root and the bud of the bud
and the sky of the sky of a tree called life;which grows
higher than soul can hope or mind can hide)
and this is the wonder that's keeping the stars apart

I carry your heart(i carry it in my heart)"

So there it is. A cottage-style home carries your heart. Its true essence is not—as we have known all along—merely in shapes or textures or colors. It is not even in flowers, fabrics, furniture, or accessories. Cottage style emerges when beloved pieces come together in a home that's been thoughtfully filled with connections to nature and to the shared history of family and friends.

This, then, is my final suggestion for you. By all means, trim and paint your rooms; collect and make beautiful things to fill them. But remember that the true secret is not in having the right stuff, it is in creating a home that carries your heart and the hearts of those you love.

As always, my best to you and yours.

Jerri

$\mathcal{I}$NDEX

Accents,
    display shelf, 102-103
    floor cloth, 96-97
    half moon mantle clock, 95
    mantle clock, 92-94
    miniature wire table and chair, 98-101
    rotating with seasons, 85
    spindle clocks, 90-95
Antoinette, Marie, 8-9
Artwork, children's, 71, 75

Bathrooms, 72-73
Bedrooms, 20-21, 50-51, 64-65, 74-75, 84-
    85, 88-89, 104-106
Benches, 38-41
Blankets,
    fleece, 62-63
    scalloped, 68-69
Bookcases, 42-43
Breakfast nooks, 22

Candles, 9, 109
    gilded candlesticks for, 118-119
    teacup, 112-113
Ceilings, 12-13
Chairs, 98-101
Chandeliers, 109, 114-116
Clocks
    half moon, 95
    mantle, 92-95
    spindle, 90-92
Cottage style,
    color, 9, 14-15, 17, 24-25, 88-89
    defined, 7-9
    planning, 12-13
    research, 10-11
    rules, 9
    scrounging for treasures, 18-19

Decoupage,
    tabletops, 28-31
    techniques, 31
Dining rooms, 12-13, 16, 89

Embellished
    bookcase, 42-43
    frame, 83
    linens, 64-69
Estate sales, 18-19

Fabric
    basket liner pillow, 58
    embellished linens, 64-69
    envelope pillow, 54-56
    fleece blanket, 62-63
    floor cloth, 96-97
    glass-top table, 26-27
    incorporating into projects, 9, 49-53
    lampshades, 117
    mirror, 78-79
    pieced pillow, 60-61
    script pillow, 59-60
    silk flower bouquet pillow, 57
Flooring, 13
    floor cloth, 96-97
Frames,
    arranging, 75
    beadboard, 80-81
    embellished, 83
    molding compound, 82-83
    oval, 126-127
Furnishings,
    all white, 24-25
    decoupage tabletop, 28-31
    drop leaf table, 34-37
    embellished bookcase, 42-43
    five-board bench, 38-41

INDEX (CONT.)

garden-themed, 9, 22-23
glass-top table, 26-27
mirrored tray table, 32-33
simple headboard, 44-47

Garage sales, 18-19

Halla-Poe, Dorothy, 9
Headboards, 44-47

Land of Oz Bed and Breakfast, 9
Lighting,
    baluster lamp, 120-121
    candles, 9, 112-113
    chandeliers, 114-116
    choosing kinds of, 109
    decorative lampshades, 117
    fading or discoloration from, 106
    gilded candlesticks, 118-119
    lamp repair, 129
    mirrors and, 108
    mood created by, 9
    refurbished chandelier, 114-116
    sunshine as, 106-107
    teacup candle, 112-113
    teapot lamp, 110-111
Lamps,
    baluster, 120-121
    choosing, 109
    making decorative lampshades for, 117
    repair of, 129
    teapot, 110-111
Linens,
    embellished, 64-69
    fleece blanket, 62-63
    pillowcases, 67
    scalloped blanket, 68-69
    scented, 49
    sheet flaps, 65-67

Mirrors,
    arranging, 72
    fabric-covered, 78-79

mosaic, 76-78
tables and, 32-33
textured, 79
Molding, 13
Mood, 9
Mosaic, 76-78

Painting tips, 25, 37
Palace of Versailles, 9
Patterns,
    enlarging and transferring, 125-126
    for projects, 130-135
Pillows,
    basket liner, 58
    choosing, 50-53
    envelope, 54-56
    fringe and, 125
    pieced, 60-61
    pillowcases, 67
    script, 59-60
    silk flower bouquet, 57
    techniques, 123-125
Planning, 12-13
Projects
    baluster lamp, 120-121
    basket liner pillow, 58
    beadboard frame, 80-81
    decoupage tabletop, 28-31
    display shelf, 102-103
    drop leaf table, 34-37
    embellished bookcase, 42-43
    embellished frame, 83
    embellished linens, 64-69
    envelope pillow, 54-56
    fabric-covered mirror, 78-79
    five-board bench, 38-41
    fleece blanket, 62-63
    floor cloth, 96-97
    gilded candlesticks, 118-119
    glass-top table, 26-27
    half moon mantle clock, 95
    making decorative lampshades, 117
    mantle clock, 92-94
    miniature wire table and chair, 98-101
    mirrored tray table, 32-33
    molding compound frame, 82-83

mosaic mirror, 76-78

painted glass table, 26-27

pieced pillow, 60-61

refurbished chandelier, 114-116

script pillow, 59-60

silk flower bouquet pillow, 57

simple headboard, 44-47

spindle clocks, 90-92

teacup candle, 112-113

teapot lamp, 110-111

textured mirror, 79

Propane torches, 127-128

Scrounging for treasures, 18-19

Shelves, 102-103

Silk flowers, 57

Sitting areas, 8, 15, 22-25, 52-53, 86-87, 106-107

Slipcovers, 21

Soldering, 127-128

Stains, removing, 50

Tables

decoupage, 28-31

drop leaf, 34-37

glass-top, 26-27

miniature wire, 98-101

mirrored tray, 32-33

painted, 26-27

Techniques, 122-129

decoupage, 31

lamp repair, 129

ovals, making, 126-127

patterns, enlarging and transferring, 125-126

pillows, 123-125

soldering, 127-128

Texture, 13, 17

beadboard frame, 80-81

embellished bookcase, 42-43

embellished frame, 83

embellished linens, 64-69

mosaic mirror, 76-78

textured mirror, 79

Themes, 7-9, 22-23, 88-89

Trends, 15

Walls, 12-13

Wicker, 86-87

Wire table and chair, 98-101

PHOTOGRAPHERS

CONTRIBUTORS

We would like to thank the following individuals and organizations for their generous support.

April Cornell
3565 Galleria
Edina, MN 55435
(952) 836-0830
www.aprilcornell.com

Apropolis
1520 East 46th Street
Minneapolis, MN 55407
(612) 827-1974
rajtarprod@worldnet.att.net

Smith & Hawken
3564 Galleria
Edina, MN 55435
(952) 285-1110
www.smithandhawken.com

Sticks & Stones Interiors
4000 Minnetonka Blvd.
Minneapolis, MN 55416
(952) 926-1567

Que Será
3580 Galleria
Edina, MN 55435
(952) 924-6390
Que Será offers vintage inspired
home furnishings, including custom
upholstery, case goods, lighting, bedding, personal & home accessories.

Oh Baby!
3515 Galleria
Edina, MN 55435
(952)928-9119

Oh Baby! on the Lake
743 E. Lake Street
Wayzata, MN 553918
(952) 404-0170
Oh Baby! and Oh Baby! on the
Lake feature the finest clothing and
accessories for infants, toddlers,
and children plus full custom furniture and bedding for boys and girls.

McCoy Pottery Collection
Courtesy of Jeanette Moss McCurdy
Stillwater, MN

Architectural Products by Outwater
22 Passaic Street
Wood-Ridge NJ 07075
(Locations also in Arizona and
    Canada)
Free Catalog Request:
1-888-772-1400
Sales & Product Info:
1-800-435-4400
www.outwater.com

Land of Oz Bed and Breakfast
N1874 670th St.
Bay City, WI 54723
(715) 594-3844
www.landofoztouristcottages.com

CREDITS

CREATIVE
PUBLISHING
international

President/CEO: Michael Eleftheriou
Vice President/Publisher: Linda Ball
Vice President/Retail Sales & Marketing:
  Kevin Haas

Executive Editor: Bryan Trandem
Editorial Director: Jerri Farris
Creative Director: Tim Himsel
Managing Editor: Michelle Skudlarek

Authors: Jerri Farris, Tim Himsel
Editor: Karen Ruth
Project Managers: Julie Caruso, Tracy Stanley
Copy Editor: Tracy Stanley
Assisting Art Director: Russ Kuepper
Mac Designer: Jon Simpson
Stock Photo Editor: Julie Caruso
Technical Photo Stylist: Teresa Henn
Creative Photo Stylist: John Rajtar
Sample Artist: Sheila Duffy
Director, Production Services & Photography: Kim Gerber
Studio Services Manager: Jeanette Moss McCurdy
Photographers: Tate Carlson, Andrea Rugg
Scene Shop Carpenter: Randy Austin
Production Manager: Stasia Dorn
Illustrator: Earl Slack
Author Portraits by: Andrea Rugg
Front Cover Photograph by: Jessie Walker

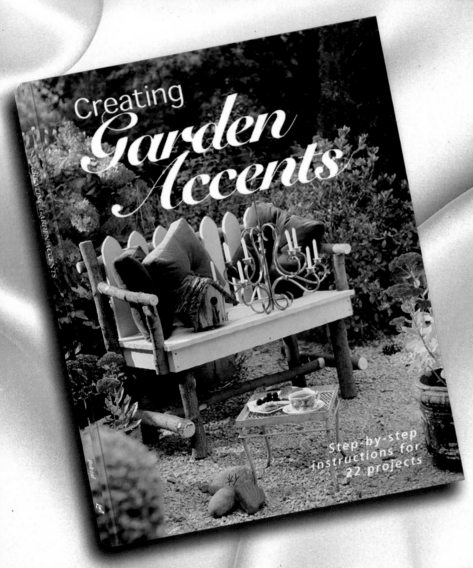